Hunter-Gatherer in
North and Central India:
An Ethnoarchaeological Approach

SOUTH ASIAN ARCHAEOLOGY SERIES

EDITED BY ALOK K. KANUNGO   No. 9

Hunter-Gatherers in North and Central India: An Ethnoarchaeological Study

Malti Nagar

Formerly Reader in Ethnoarchaeology, Dept. of Archaeology
Deccan College Post-Graduate & Research Institute, Pune – 411006, INDIA

BAR International Series 1749
2008

Published in 2016 by
BAR Publishing, Oxford

BAR International Series 1749

South Asian Archaeology Series No. 9
Series Editor: Alok K. Kanungo

Hunter-Gatherers in North and Central India: An Ethnoarchaeological Study

ISBN 978 1 4073 0209 6

© M Nagar and the Publisher 2008

The author's moral rights under the 1988 UK Copyright,
Designs and Patents Act are hereby expressly asserted.

All rights reserved. No part of this work may be copied, reproduced, stored,
sold, distributed, scanned, saved in any form of digital format or transmitted
in any form digitally, without the written permission of the Publisher.

BAR Publishing is the trading name of British Archaeological Reports (Oxford) Ltd.
British Archaeological Reports was first incorporated in 1974 to publish the BAR
Series, International and British. In 1992 Hadrian Books Ltd became part of the BAR
group. This volume was originally published by John and Erica Hedges Ltd. in
conjunction with British Archaeological Reports (Oxford) Ltd / Hadrian Books Ltd, the
Series principal publisher, in 2008. This present volume is published by BAR
Publishing, 2016.

Printed in England

PUBLISHING

BAR titles are available from:

          BAR Publishing
          122 Banbury Rd, Oxford, OX2 7BP, UK
EMAIL   info@barpublishing.com
PHONE +44 (0)1865 310431
FAX   +44 (0)1865 316916
          www.barpublishing.com

About the Book

India has a long history of hunting-gathering, nomadic way of life going back to the Lower Palaeolithic period, about a million years ago. It continued through the Middle and Upper Palaeolithic, with steady improvement in technology and social organization. The Mesolithic period which lasted from about 10,000 years ago till well after the emergence of agriculture about 6000 years ago, witnessed significant improvement in technology which was based on the mass production of bladelets and their conversion into microliths by blunting one or more margins. The microliths were hafted into bone and wooden handles and shafts to produce spearheads, arrowheads, knives, daggers, harpoons, etc. which were used for hunting, cutting carcasses and making wooden tools. This way of life is known from almost all over the country, except the greater part of the Ganga plain and north-east India. It is well documented at more than thirty excavated Mesolithic sites which have yielded stone tools and animal remains, and in a few cases burials with human skeletal remains.

Paintings found in a large number of caves and rock shelters, specially in central India, complement the picture of hunting-gathering way of life known from the excavation of living floors in caves, rock shelters and open-air sites.

Settled life based on agriculture and stone and copper technology appeared around six thousand years ago and was slowly adopted by most of the Mesolithic communities. However, the farmers did not give up hunting-gathering altogether and continued to practise it in some measure. Even after the appearance of iron technology hunting continued to be practised and indeed it has survived right into the twenty-first century among many communities all over the country, including in the densely populated Indo-Gangetic plains. Some of the well-known living hunting-gathering communities are the Bhils, Van Vgaris and Kal Beliyas in Rajasthan; Pardhis and Kuchbandhias in Madhya Pradesh; Pardhis in Maharashtra; Kanjars, Sansis, Haburas. Berias, Baheliyas and other groups in the Ganga plains; Paharias, Mankadias and Birhors in eastern India, Chenchus, Yanadis and Yerukulas in the Eastern Ghats, and Kadars and Cholanaikams in Kerala.

This book comprehensively documents the hunting-gathering way of life in India from the Lower Palaeolithic to the present. It is based on the author's field work in Rajasthan, Madhya Pradesh and Uttar Pradesh, and published archaeological and ethnographic evidence from these regions.

To

My Teachers

V.N. Misra & H.D. Sankalia

Foreword

Alok Kumar Kanungo
Series Editor, South Asian Archaeology Series
International Series of British Reports

The International Series of British Archaeological Reports, with its 1700 titles to the present time, is undoubtedly one of the most important places of publication in the discipline of Archaeology. But it is a pity that works on the archaeology of South Asia have been less represented in the series than their interest and value deserves.

The archaeological record of South Asia (comprising India, Pakistan, Nepal, Bhutan, Bangladesh, Sri Lanka and the Maldives) is extremely rich. This wealth begins in the Lower Palaeolithic period and includes, for example, the Harappan Civilization, one of the oldest in the world (covering a very large area and having many unique features -- the most ancient known town planning, its architecture and high standards of civic hygiene, its art, iconography, paleography, numismatics and international trade). South Asia also has a large number of earlier, contemporary, and later Neolithic and Chalcolithic cultures. Moreover, what makes South Asia particularly significant for the study of past human behaviour is the survival of many traditional modes of life, like hunting-gathering, pastoralism, shifting cultivation, fishing, and fowling, the study of which throws valuable light on the reconstruction of past cultures. In the region there are a large number of government and semi-government institutions devoted to archaeological teaching and/or research in archaeology and a large and professionally trained body of researchers.

Of course, a number of universities and other institutions, in the area do have their own publication programmes and there are also reputed private publishing houses. However, British Archaeological Reports, a series of 30 years standing, has an international reputation and distribution system. In order to take advantage of the latter – to bring archaeological researches in South Asia to the notice of scholars in the western academic world – the South Asian Archaeology Series has been instituted within the International Series of British Archaeological Reports. This series (which it is hoped to associate with an institution of organization in the area) aims at publishing original research works of international interest in all branches of archaeology of South Asia.

Those wishing to submit books for inclusion in the South Asian Archaeology Series should contact the South Asian Archaeology Series Editor, who will mediate with BAR in Oxford. The subject has to be appropriate and of the correct academic standard (*curriculum vitae* are requested and books may be referred); instructions for formatting will be given, as necessary.

Dr. Alok Kumar Kanungo
Department of Archaeology
Deccan College Post-Graduate & Research Institute
Pune 411006, INDIA
email: alok_kanungo@yahoo.com

Preface

During 1963-1965 I did field work among the various castes of Ahar and other nearby villages of Udaipur district in Rajasthan to collect material on traditional pottery shapes, functions, and manufacturing techniques, metal ornaments and their manufacture, domestic architecture, food habits, dress, social organization, religious beliefs and practices, and other aspects of rural life. There were two aims behind this work; one, to use this data for reconstructing the Chalcolithic culture as revealed by the material remains excavated from the site of Ahar, and ceramics collected by me from several Ahar culture sites in Udaipur and Chittaurgarh districts, and two, to find out if any of the Chalcolithic traits had survived in the present-day life, both rural and urban, of the region. As the faunal remains from Ahar included bones, teeth, etc. of both domesticated and wild animals, it was obvious that hunting had been a part of the subsistence economy of the Ahar culture. I therefore decided to collect material on hunting-gathering practices also. Since Gametis, as Bhils settled in villages are known, were a part of the population of these villages, I also got interested in understanding the process of assimilation of the Bhils in the Hindu-dominated rural society.

During the field work I got an opportunity to visit Gogunda, known as a major pottery making centre, and some other nearby predominantly Bhil-inhabited villages in the Aravalli hills, and collected information on traditional pottery and terracotta idol making technology as well as on hunting practices and techniques of the Bhils. Later on in the 1970s and 1980s I conducted field work for many years among the Maria and Muria Gonds, Dhurwas and other tribal communities in Bastar district of Madhya Pradesh. The aim of the field work was to understand the life of the tribal peoples, particularly the use of wild plants for food, drink, medicine and other purposes, social organization, religion, and raising of stone, wood, and brick and cement memorials for the dead by the Gonds.

Between 1973 and 1977 I participated in the excavation of the rock shelters containing Palaeolithic and Mesolithic habitation deposits and Mesolithic and later paintings at Bhimbetka in Sehore district, M.P. by V.S. Wakankar and V.N. Misra, and collected data about the use of wild plant foods, hunting techniques, raising of miniature stone memorials for the dead, religion, etc. among the Gonds of Bhiyanpur and other villages near Bhimbetka. During 1988-1990 I took part in the excavation of the Palaeolithic site of Samnapur in Narsinghpur district by S.N. Rajaguru and V.N. Misra and was able to collect very interesting material on the hunting practices, technology and techniques, social organization and religion of the predominantly hunting community of Pardhis living in Chandarpura, Umrari and Anvaria villages of Sagar district, and a temporary forest camp near Samnapur. Bijai Singh, A Kuchbandhia, another predominatly hunting community, who, along with his wife, was camping near Samnapur provided very valuable information about his community.

And finally, between 1994 and 2000 I was able to make several trips to Balathal, a Chalcolithic and Iron Age site in Udaipur district, which was being excavated by V.N. Misra, V.S. Shinde and R.K. Mohanty of the Deccan College, and Lalit Pandey and J.S. Kharakwal of the Rajasthan Vidyapeeth, Udaipur. During these trips I was able to collect material on the folk religion and social organization of the Garis (shepherds), Gametis, Rabaris / Raikas (camel, sheep and goat breeders), Dangis, Gujars, Meghwals and Kal Beliyas of Balathal and its satellite hamlets. The Kal Beliyas are a nomadic community of hunters, snake catchers and snake charmers. Some of them have been settled by the State government in a colony near the village of Karanpur which is located between Udaipur airport and Vallabhnagar town. During my two visits to the colony the Kal Beliya men and women provided valuable information about their hunting practices, social organization and religion. The Gametis and Meghwals, who mainly work as labourers for farmers of more prosperous castes like Rajputs, Jats, Dangis and Gujars, still occasionally hunt small game like hare, porcupine and monitor lizard using nets and traps..

In 1995 the Indian Council of Historical Research (ICHR) gave me a Senior Fellowship to work on the existing hunter-gatherers of north and central India. The fellowship enabled me to make three trips to Bastar to update the data that I had collected in my earlier spells of field work and several trips to Balathal. The fellowship also enabled me to read recent literature on hunter-gatherers and organize the data I had collected over the years.

I would like to express my gratitude to many people who have provided me encouragement and help over the years in field work and preparation of this study. First of all I am indebted to my research supervisor, the late Professor H.D. Sankalia who asked me to work on an ethnoarchaeological study of the Ahar culture and inculcated in me an interest in ethnoarchaeology and the study of hunting-gathering and rural communities. Professor V.N. Misra who taught me Prehistoric Archaeology at Lucknow University, has always source of inspiration. He provided me facilities of his excavation camps at Bhimbetka, Samnapur and Balathal for carrying out field work in the villages in the vicinity of these sites. He has also allowed me to incorporate his work on the Van Vagris in this report. I am grateful to him for reading the text and making useful suggestions. I am obliged to many informants for providing information about the various aspects of the culture of their communities. I am thankful to the staff of the Deccan College library for their help in consulting books and journals. I am grateful to Dr. Alok Kumar Kanungo and Dr. Shahida Ansari for scanning drawings and photographs from published sources and for preparing the press copy. Dr. Kanungo actually took the responsibility of getting the report published. I am thankful to Dr. Shanti Pappu for help in many ways. And finally I am grateful to the ICHR for providing me a fellowship which made this study possible.

Dr. Malti Nagar
Flat No. 18, Building No. 8
Ekta Apartment, Tank Road
Vishrantwadi, Pune – 411006
INDIA

Makar Shankranti
2008

Contents

	Page No.
Preface	I-II
Contents	III-V
Antiquity of Hunting-Gathering Way of Life	1-7
1. Introduction	1-1
2. Mesolithic Sites with Faunal Remains	1-3
3. Origins of Agriculture	3-5
a. Neolithic Sites	4-5
b. Chalcolithic Sites	5-5
4. Emergence of Iron Technology and its Impact on Agriculture and Society	5-6
5. Ethnographic Studies on Hunter-Gatherers	6-7
Ganga Plains	8-26
1. Geographical Background	8-9
2. Occupational History	9-9
3. Sources of Information	9-10
4. Ethnic Groups	10-11
5. Population and Distribution	11-14
6. Settlement pattern	14-15
7. Subsistence	15-17
a. Hunting, Trapping and Fishing	15-16
b. Technology and Techniques of Hunting	16-17
c. Gathering	17-17
8. Other Occupations	17-18
9. Crime	18-20
10. Attitude of the Government	20-21
11. Interaction with Larger Society	21-25
12. Assimilation into the Caste Society	25-25
13. Conclusion	25-26
Kanjars	27-40
1. Introduction	27-28
2. Environmental Setting	28-29
3. Data and its Sources	29-29
4. Distribution	29-30
5. Settlement Pattern	30-31
6. Physical Appearance, Dress and Ornaments	31-31
7. Social Organization	31-32
8. Subsistence	32-32

9.	Technology and Techniques of Hunting	32-35
10.	Other Occupations	35-36
11.	Crime	36-36
12.	Disposal of the Dead	36-36
13.	Religion	36-37
14.	Acculturation	37-38
15.	Recent Changes	38-39
16.	Relevance for Social History	39-39
17.	Conclusion	39-40

Rajasthan 41-61

1.	Introduction	41-43
2.	Van Vagris	43-58
	2.1 Are the Van Vagris an Independent Group?	43-46
	2.2 Sources of Data	46-47
	2.3 Habitat, Demography and Settlement Pattern	47-49
	2.4 Physical Appearance, Dress and Ornaments	49-50
	2.5 Temperament and Character	50-50
	2.6 Social organization	50-51
	2.7 Marriage	51-51
	2.8 Subsistence and Economy	51-53
	2.9 Hunting Technology and techniques	53-55
	2.10 Religion	55-57
	2.11 Relationship with other Communities	57-57
	2.12 Relationship with Politico-Administrative System	57-58
	2.13 Future Prospects	58-58
3.	Bhils	58-60
4.	Kal Beliyas	60-61

Central India 62-89

1.	Geographical Setting	62-62
2.	Pardhis	62-86
	2.1 Sources of Information	63-64
	2.2 Settlements and Camps	64-65
	2.2.1 Chandarpura	65-66
	2.2.2 Umrari	66-66
	2.2.3 Aanvaria	66-66
	2.2.4 Forest Camp near Samnapur	66-67
	2.3 Informants	67-67
	2.4 Distribution and Population	67-69
	2.5 Settlement pattern	69-70
	2.6 Composition of Settlements and Camps	70-70
	2.7 Language	70-71
	2.8 Dress and Appearance	71-71
	2.9 Social Organization	71-73

2.10 Marriage and Family	73-74
2.11 Disposal of the Dead	74-75
2.12 Religion	75-76
2.13 Economy	77-77
2.13.1 Hunting	77-78
2.13.2 Hunting Technology and Techniques	78-83
2.13.3 Trade	83-84
2.13.4 Animal Husbandry, Agriculture and other Occupations	84-84
2.14 Crime	84-85
2.15 Panchayat	85-85
2.16 Economic and Social Change	85-86
3. Kuchbandhias	86-89
3.1 Social Organization	87-87
3.2 Religion	87-87
3.3 Hunting	87-88
3.4 Other Occupations	88-88
3.5 Change	88-89
4. Bawarias	89-89

Significance of Hunting-Foraging Lifeways for Interpretation of Archaeological Data — 90-99

1.1 Ganga Plains	90-94
1.2 Rajasthan	94-97
1.3 Central India	97-99

Bibliography — 100-103

About Author — 104-104

ANTIQUITY OF HUNTING-GATHERING WAY OF LIFE

1. Introduction

Humans are descended from apes similar to chimpanzee and gorilla and like their ancestors the earliest humans were vegetarians. However, at some stage they started consuming meat. Initially they were able to hunt only small animals and were probably scavenging flesh from carnivore kills. It is believed that *Homo erectus* started hunting large game like wild cattle, antelope, deer, elephant, and rhinoceros, but even at that stage scavenging is thought to have been the major source of his meat supply. The Neanderthal people of the Middle Palaeolithic period were definitely hunting large game as shown by the bones and teeth of animals and wear marks on the flint projectile points found at the archaeological sites. From the Upper Palaeolithic period there is additional evidence of hunting in the form of depiction of hunting scenes in cave paintings. However, during all this long period wild plant foods like leaves, flowers, fruits, seeds and roots must have been the main source of food because their availability was more assured than that of game animals since plants cannot move. Also, collecting plant foods was less strenuous than hunting.

In India fossilized bones of a variety of wild animals like cattle, buffalo, elephant, rhinoceros, hippopotamus, antelope, deer, and pig have been found in abundance in association with Palaeolithic tools in the alluvial deposits of a number of rivers like the Yamuna, Belan, Son, Mahanadi, Narmada, Godavari, Manjhra, Pravara, Ghod, Krishna, Tungabhadra and their tributaries. However, there is no clear evidence that these animals were hunted by man. Probably hunter-gatherers scavenged the flesh of animals which died a natural death or were killed by predators.

2. Mesolithic Sites with Faunal Remains

The Mesolithic people, however, were definitely practising hunting because the ones of a variety of small and large animals have been found in stratified context and in association with a variety of cultural materials at the excavated sites of Langhnaj in Gujarat, Bagor and Tilwara in Rajasthan, Adamgarh and Bhimbetka in Madhya Pradesh, and Lekhahia, Morhana Pahar, Baghai Khor, Sarai Nahar Rai, Mahadaha, Damdama and Chopani Mando in Uttar Pradesh (Clutton-Brock 1965; Sharma 1973; Sharma *et al.* 1980; Thomas 1984; Thomas *et al.* 2002; Joglekar *et al.* 2003). The wild fauna found at individual Mesolithic sites comprises the following species:

Langhnaj
Rhinoceros (*Rhinoceros unicornis*), Boar (*Sus scrofa*), Nilgai (*Boselaphus tragocamelus*), Blackbuck (*Antilope cervicapra*), Chinkara (*Gazella dorcas*), rasingha (*Cervus duvauceli*), Sambar (*Cervus unicoor*), Chital (*Axis axis*), Hog deer (*Axis porcinus*), Wolf (*Canis lupus*), Fox (*Vulpes bengalensis*), Mongoose (*Herpestes edwardsi*), Hare (*Lepus nigrocollis*), Squirrel (*Funambulus* sp.), Tortoise, Yellow monitor (*Varanus flavescens*), and fish.

Tilwara
Chital (*Axis axis*), Hog deer. (*Axis porcinus*) and Mongoose (*Herpestes edwardsi*).

Bagor
Nilgai (*Boselaphus tragocamelus*), Blackbuck (*Antilope cervicapra*), Chinkara *Gazella dorcas*), Barasingha (*Cervus duvauceli*), Chital (*Axis axis*), Fox (*Vulpes bengalensis*), Mongoose (*Herpestes edwardsi*), and Hare (*Lepus nigrocollis*).

Adamgarh
Chital (*Axis axis*), Hare (*Lepus nigrocollis*), Squirrel (*Funambulus* sp.), and Yellow monitor (*Varanus flavescens*).

Sarai Nahar Rai
Cattle (*Bos* sp.), (Buffalo (*Bubalus arnee*), Elephant (*Elephas maximus*), and tortoise.

Mahadaha
Cattle (*Bos* sp.), Gaur (*Bos gaurus*), Buffalo (*Bubalus arnee*), Nilgai (*Boselaphus tragocamelus*), Goat (*Capra* sp.),Chital (*Axis axis*), Hog deer (*Axis porcinus*), Sambar / Barasingha (*Cervus* sp.), Barking Deer (*Muntiacus muntjac*), Small Deer, Chousingha (*Tetracerus quadricornis*), Blackbuck (*Antilope cervicapra*), Chinkara (*Gazella bennetti*), Boar (*Sus srofa*), Pigmy Hog (*Sus salvanius*), Hippopotamus (*Hippopotamus* sp.), Wolf (*Canis lupus*), Jackal (*Canis aureus*), Jungle Cat (*Felis chaus*), Mongoose (*Herpestes edwardsi*), Porcupine (*Hystrix indica*), House Rat (*Rattus rattus*), Rhinoceros (*Rhinoceros unicornis*), Elephant (*Elephas maximus*), and Hare (*Lepus nigrocollis*). Besides, bones of several birds, including Crane, Heron, Duck/Teal (*Anas* sp.), Ganges Softshell turtle (*Tryonix gangeticus*), Indian Flapshell turtle (*Lissemys punctata*), Indian Sawback turtle (*Kanchuga tecta*), Common Indian Monitor lizard (*Varanus bengalensis*), Indian Marsh crocodile (*Crocodylus palustris*), Freshwater fish and Freshwater mussel, have also been found.

Damdama
The fauna from Damdama is fairly similar to that from Mahadaha which is to be expected as both the sites are located in the same environment. It includes the following species:

Cattle (*Bos* sp.), Gaur (*Bos gaurus*), Buffalo (*Bubalus arnee*), Goat (*Capra* sp.) Chital (*Axis axis*), Hog deer (*Axis porcinus*), Sambar / Barasingha (*Cervus* sp.), Barking Deer (*Muntiacus muntjac*), *Moschus moschiferus*, *Tragulus memina*, Nilgai (*Boselaphus tragocamelus*), Chowsingha (*Tetracerus quadricornis*), Blackbuck (*Antilope cervicapra*), Chinkara (*Gazella bennetti*), Boar (*Sus srofa*), Pigmy Hog (*Sus salvanius*), Wolf (*Canis lupus*), Jackal (*Canis aureus*), Fox (*Vulpes bengalensis*), Sloth bear (*Melurus ursinus*), Mongoose (*Herpestes edwardsi*), Porcupine (*Hystrix indica*), House Rat (*Rattus rattus*), Rhinoceros (*Rhinoceros unicornis*), Elephant (*Elephas maximus*), *Gallus gallus*, Ganges Softshell turtle (*Tryonix gangeticus*), Indian Flapshell turtle (*Lissemys punctata*), *Chitra indica*, *Varanus* sp. *Calotes versicolor*, *Pila globosa*), Freshwater fish and Freshwater mussel.

The percentage of different classes of animals in the faunal assemblage is as follows: Mammals (77.39), Reptiles (12.1), Birds (8.96), Fish (1.20), and Molluscs (0.30).

Bhimbetka
Rhinoceros (*Rhinoceros unicornis*), Sambar (*Cervus unicolor*), and Chital (*Axis axis*).

At all the sites bones are frequently found in a charred condition, suggesting that animal flesh was roasted on open fires. The bones are mostly fragmentary, showing that they were broken and split open to extract the marrow.

The evidence from faunal remains is supplemented by that from rock paintings. Several thousand painted rockshelters are known from the Vindhyan sandstone region of central India. The main subject matter of the paintings is wild animals. These comprise Indian humped cattle, gaur, buffalo, nilgai, sambar, chital, boar, rhinoceros, monkey, and rat. The animals are shown being hunted by individual hunters as well as by groups of hunters.

The hunters use spears, bow and arrow and a variety of nets and traps. There are also scenes of rats being dug out from their holes by digging sticks. In addition, there are frequent scenes of fishing by nets and traps as well as by bow and arrow, and of collection of fruits from trees and of honey from beehives.

The life of the Mesolithic hunter-gatherers was nomadic but only partially. The thick habitation deposits in rock shelters as well as at some open air sites and particularly the presence of cemeteries with large number of graves at sites like Sarai Nahar Rai, Mahadaha and Damdama shows that human groups were living at one place for several months. However, as different plant foods are available only seasonally and animals also have to move in search of food and water, particularly during summer months, people may not have always stayed at one place throughout the year.

3. Origins of Agriculture

Hunting-gathering groups had been watching the behaviour of plants and animals for hundreds of generations and had slowly acquired an intimate knowledge of their behaviour. They must have found out which plants have edible parts and which plants flower and give fruits in which season. Similarly, they must have learnt which animals are harmless and can be easily approached, and in which season they give birth to babies. This accumulated knowledge ultimately culminated into cultivation of plants and domestication of animals. This change, which had far reaching consequences for the future of human society, first took place around ten thousand years ago in the Near and Middle East, i.e. the land lying between the eastern shore of the Mediterranean sea and the eastern edge of the Baluchistan plateau. This is because the first plants to be cultivated by man, namely wheat and barley, were growing in a wild state in this region, and the first animals to be domesticated, namely cattle, sheep and goat, were also roaming wild in this region.

Once people learnt to cultivate plants and domesticate animals, they had assured food supply. The harvested cereals and pulses could be stored for many months, and animals could be slaughtered as and when meat was required. With assured food supply people could stay permanently at one place provided water was available all the year round. Thus, life became settled and villages came into existence. The hunter-gatherer groups realized the enormous benefits of the farming way of life, and more and more of them adopted it.

With assured food supply, population began to increase dramatically, and new settlements had to be founded. Some enterprising farmers were able to produce more food than they needed for themselves and their families, and so they could share it with others. Thus it was not necessary for all the members of a group or community to be engaged in food production. Those individuals who were not directly engaged in agricultural activities could devote their talents and energies to other tasks like production of craft items like pottery, implements of wood required for agricultural activities and furniture, items of rope, beads of semi-precious stones and terracotta, bricks, stone quarrying, and masonry. Items of surplus craft production could be supplied to other communities, and raw materials not locally available could be procured from other places. Thus, trade came into existence and the society became divided into farmers, craftsmen and traders. Eventually, villages grew into towns and towns into cities, and finally around five-and-a-half thousand years ago the first civilizations of the world, namely those of the valleys of the Nile in Egypt, Tigris and Euphrates in Mesopotamia (modern Iraq), and the Indus in South Asia emerged.

From the Near East and West Asia the knowledge of agriculture and associated way of life diffused to Europe, Africa and South Asia. One of the many consequences of food production was a dramatic growth in human population. Others were deforestation due to clearing of vegetation, soil erosion, and floods. In the Indian subcontinent the oldest known village, dated to about seven thousand years ago, is Mehrgarh, located on the bank of the Bolan river, a tributary of the Indus, in eastern Baluchistan. As the narrow valleys of the Baluchistan plateau were unable to accommodate the expanding population, some of it migrated to the Indus valley which had vast, fertile and well-watered land. Agriculture-based settlements began to appear in the Indus valley and as population grew, new settlements were founded. And in due course Indus or Harappan civilization emerged in this area.

The Indus/ Harappan Civilization, characterized by cities, towns and villages, flourished in the valleys of the Indus and its tributaries and those of the Sarasvati, which flowed parallel to, and east of the Indus. The eastern limit of this civilization was the Ganga river which it never crossed. In part contemporary but largely successive to the Indus civilization, rural settlements marked by agriculture and simple mud, mud-brick or stone houses, were appearing in other parts of India. These settlements are grouped into two broad cultural categories, namely Neolithic and Chalcolithic, the difference between the two being mainly technological. The technology of the Neolithic cultures consisted of ground stone tools like axes, adzes and chisels, and stone blades and microliths. The last made by blunting one or more margins of tiny blades or microblades were hafted into bone and wooden handles to make sickles, knives, daggers, arrowheads, and spearheads. The technology of the Chalcolithic cultures consisted of stone blade tools and copper tools. The people of both culture groups were practising domestication of animals and cultivation of plant crops.

The Neolithic cultures mainly flourished in the Kashmir valley, Vindhyan plateau region, South India, eastern India and northeastern India while the Chalcolithic cultures flourished in Mewar or southeast Rajasthan, middle and lower Ganga valley, eastern part of Gujarat, Malwa or western Madhya Pradesh, and western Maharashtra or northern Deccan.

Even though the subsistence economy of both Neolithic and Chalcolithic cultures was based on agriculture, the people did not entirely give up hunting and probably gathering as well. A large number of Neolithic and Chalcolithic sites have been excavated, and every single excavated site has yielded skeletal remains of wild animals, and in many cases of birds and aquatic creatures like fish and turtles as well. The major Neolithic and Chalcolithic sites which have been excavated are listed below region-wise:

3.1 Neolithic sites

Kashmir valley: 1. Burzahom, 2. Gufkral

Vindhyan Region: 1. Koldihwa, 2. Mahagara, 3. Tokwa, 4. Senuwar

South India: 1. Maski, 2. Brahmagiri, 3. Piklihal, 4. Utnur, 5. Paiyampalli, 6. Sangankallu, 7. Tekkalakota, 8. Hallur,

9. Ramapuram, 10. Veerapuram, 11. Palavoy, 12. Kodekal, 13. Budihal, 14. T. Narsipur

3.2 Chalcolithic Sites

Mewar: 1. Ahar, 2. Gilund, 3. Balathal, 4. Ojiyana, 5. Lachhura

Ganga Valley: 1. Sohgaura, 2. Narhan, 3. Khairadih, 4. Imlidih Khurd, 5. Dhuriapar, 6. Waina, 7. Bhunadih, 8. Malhar, 9. Agiabir, 10. Jhusi, 11. Dadupur, 12. Lahuradewa, 13. Hetapatti in Uttar Pradesh; 14. Chirand, 15. Chechar Kutubpur, 16. Taradih in Bihar, 17. Mahisadal, 18. Pandu Rajar Dhibi, and 19. Mangalkot in West Bengal.

Malwa: 1. Navdatoli, 2. Eran, 3. Nagda, 4. Kayatha, 5. Azadnagar, and 6. Dhangwada

Maharashtra: 1. Jorwe, 2. Nevasa, 3. Daimabad, 4. Kaothe, 5. Prakashe, 6. Bahal, 7. Apegaon, 8. Chandoli, 9. Songaon, 10.Inamgaon, and 11. Walki

Each of these sites has yielded remains of wild animals. It will be repetitive and wastage of space to list the remains from each site individually because for the most part they are common to all the sites. The faunal remains mainly represent cattle, buffalo, sambar, chital, barasingha, chowsingha, hog deer, barking deer, nilgai, blackbuck, fox, boar, wolf, jackal, hare, porcupine, mongoose, monitor lizard, several kinds of birds, fishes and turtles.

4. Emergence of Iron Technology and its Impact on Agriculture and Society

Toward the end of the second millennium B.C. iron technology appeared in India and it quickly replaced the copper-bronze and stone tool technology. Copper and bronze are brittle metals and were always scarce, and hence tools made of these materials were available only to some people. Also, axes and other tools made of these metals as well as of stone were not effective for clearing dense vegetation of the sub-humid and humid regions. In contrast, iron was plentifully available and hence tools and weapons made of this metal became available to every one. Iron tools were also more sturdy and therefore more effective in clearing dense vegetation. With the introduction of iron technology clearance of primeval vegetation for creating land for farming and settlement in zones of high rainfall got a new momentum. Agricultural operations also became more efficient and faster with the help of iron tools. With the increased productivity of agriculture population growth was also accelerated, and therefore more and more forest land was brought under cultivation. This process is still continuing and we have now reached a stage when virtually no forest may survive in a few decades.

As forests diminished, so did wildlife. With the increasing depletion of wild plant and animal food resources hunter-gatherer groups were forced to give up their traditional way of life and take to agriculture and other occupations. However, some groups were either too conservative or too lazy to change, and have persisted with their traditional way of life right into the twenty-first century, and it will probably take several decades before this atavistic way of life disappears altogether. Perhaps one reason for the long survival of this way of life is the freedom it gives to its practitioners. While farmers have to toil for most of the year and for many hours every day to produce surplus food and other agricultural produce to enjoy the benefits of farming, hunting-gathering does not make heavy demands of hard work on its followers. Hunter-gatherers live from day to day; they have limited material possessions and do not aspire for more. Hunting-gathering does not demand fixed and regular hours of work. A hunter-gatherer may go for hunting or plant food collecting as and when he feels hungry or is inclined to hunt or gather food. At worst he may have to go hungry to sleep but he is under no compulsion of a fixed work schedule like the farmer and other categories of workers in modern society.

5. Ethnographic Studies on Hunter-Gatherers

References to hunter-gatherers occur throughout our literature. The Nishadas, Bhillas, Saoras, etc. who are mentioned in the *Ramayana* and the *Mahabharata* were almost certainly practising hunting-gathering. At the end of the Mahabharata *war* Shri Krishna was shot by the arrow of a Bhilla or Bhil. References to hunter-gatherers occur in Banbhatta's *Harshacharita* and other historical works.

However, it was the British administrators who began a systematic survey and documentation of all the Indian communities, including the hunter-gatherers, from the beginning of the nineteenth century. Brief accounts of all the castes and tribes were collected and published in these ethnographic surveys. The well-known regional accounts of castes and tribes are those of Denzil Ibbetson (1916) on the Punjab, of William Crooke (1896) on the North Western Provinces and Oudh, i.e. present-day Uttar Pradesh, of E.T. Dalton (1872) on Bengal, i.e. the present-day states of West Bengal, Bihar and Orissa, of R.E. Enthoven (1920, 1922) on Bombay Presidency, of R.V. Russell and R.B. Hira Lal (1916) on central India, of E. Thurston (1909) on south India, and of L.K.A.K. Iyer (1909-1912) on Cochin, a part of the present-day State of Kerala.

Valuable information about hunter-gatherer communities is to be found in the ethnographic studies by J. C. Nesfield (1883) on the Kanjars of north India, by S.C. Roy (1912, 1915, 1925) on the tribes of Chota Nagpur, by Fuerer-Haimendorf (1943) on the Chenchus, by D.N. Majumdar (1944) on the tribes of the hilly region of the Mirzapur district of Uttar Pradesh and Chhota Nagpur, by Verrier Elwin (1939, 1947, 1950) on the tribes of central India and Orissa, by T.B. Naik (1956) on the Bhils, by Stephen Fuchs (1986) on the Korkus of the Vindhya Hills, by K.C. Malhotra and his colleagues (1983) on the Phanse Pardhis and other groups in Maharashtra, and many others. Very useful information about the hunter-gatherers is also available in District Gazetteers and Census reports.

Because of the creation of farmland to support the steadily growing population and establishment of human settlements, including schools, colleges, playgrounds, parks, hospitals, banks, etc., building of roads, railways, airports, etc., digging of canals, establishments of factories, and creation of various other facilities more and more forest had to be cleared. In this process resources for the subsistence of the hunter-gatherers were depleted. They were therefore forced to look for supplementary resources and occupations for their living. Also, with the shrinking of their habitat the hunter-gatherers were obliged to live in close proximity to villages and towns. They used their intimate knowledge of the resources of their environment and traditional craft skills of making hunting and fishing gear to produce a variety of craft items from grass, string, stone, etc. which were required by the farmers. They also supplied the flesh of wild animals and birds as well as honey to village and town people. Some groups took to providing entertainment to rural and city people through music and dance.

In this way the hunter-gatherers have tried to establish a symbiotic relationship with the settled population. However, this relationship occasionally involves clash of interest and leads to conflict between the farmers and hunter-gatherers. With forest mostly gone the hunter-gatherers often hunt small game like jackal, fox, hare, porcupine, monitor lizard and birds in the fields of the farmers which the latter resent, particularly if they happen to have strong feelings against violence as many people in Rajasthan and Gujarat, where there is a strong influence of Jainism, do. Most of the hunter-gatherers also took to crime like committing theft and robbery for their survival. In many ways their plight is very similar to that of the wild animals like lions, tigers, panthers, hyenas and wolves, which, because of the steady depletion of the forest and their prey base of wild herbivores, start killing the livestock in the villages and towns and occasionally even human beings. The studies of the selected hunter-gatherer communities presented in the ensuing chapters clearly illustrate this unfortunate situation (Fig. 1).

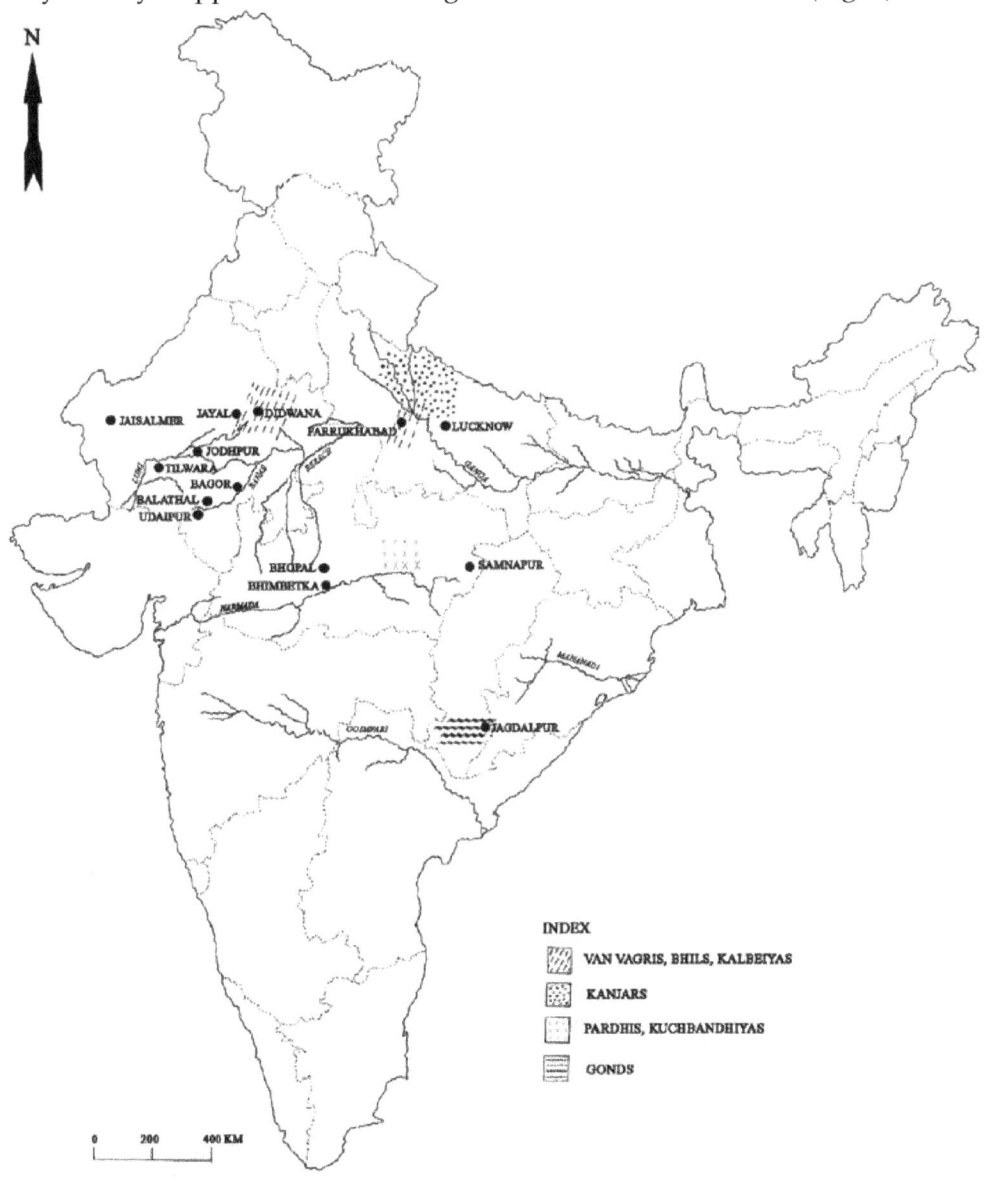

Fig. 1. Areas of study

GANGA PLAINS

India has a tribal population of over sixty million people comprising more than three hundred distinct communities which are officially designated as 'Scheduled Tribes' for favoured treatment in their educational and economic development. These tribal communities are mainly confined to the hilly and forested regions of the country, like the Aravalli, Vindhya and Satpura Hills, Western and Eastern Ghats, Chota Nagpur plateau, and northeast India outside the Bramhaputra Valley. As the topography of these regions makes them unsuitable for large-scale irrigation-based agriculture and for smooth transport and communication, they did not attract advanced agriculturists until the pressure of population in the more favourable alluvial plains forced farming groups to move into these less attractive environments in search of arable land. The tribal or aboriginal communities were therefore able to preserve their traditional modes of subsistence (hunting-gathering, fishing, shifting cultivation, and primitive plough cultivation), and their linguistic and cultural identities.

The establishment of British rule in the country in the eighteenth century initiated a new phase in the opening up of tribal habitats to outsiders. Systematic exploitation of forest and mineral resources, setting up of industries, development of rail and road communications, and rapid increase in human population in the plains subsequent to the improvement of law and order, expansion in medical facilities and general economic development, all contributed to the acceleration of this process. It has been further intensified by the planned development activities initiated after Independence. As a result, tribal cultures have suffered much disintegration and impoverishment, and today there are hardly any areas in which these cultures survive in their pristine purity.

Against this background one would have thought that at least in the intensively cultivated and densely populated alluvial plains the aboriginal groups practising pre-agricultural or hunting-foraging mode of subsistence would have been completely assimilated into the new socio-cultural order. But in fact this has not always been the case. A good illustration of such a situation can be seen in the upper and middle Ganga plain.

1. Geographical Background

The upper and middle Ganga plain (77 and 84 E : 25 and 30 N) is administratively broadly equivalent to the present day State of Uttar Pradesh. In pre-Independence days this region was successively known as North-Western Provinces and Oudh, and United Provinces of Agra and Oudh. Geographically it forms a part of the vast Indo-Gangetic plain of north India which is the most fertile and densely populated region in the country. The elevation of the plain above sea level, in the region under consideration, ranges from 275 m in the west to 60 m in the east. The plain is drained by the Ganga and its numerous tributaries, some rising in the Himalayas to the north and others in the low hills of the peninsula to the south. The annual average rainfall ranges from around 800 mm in the west to around 1300 mm in the east. The natural vegetation cover is typical of the tropical dry deciduous woodlands. Steadily increasing population pressure and consequent human manipulation of the landscape over the last about six millennia, and particularly during the last couple of centuries, have almost completely obliterated the primary vegetation cover; today only a few characteristic plant species survive in heavily degraded and isolated pockets. However, even as late as fifty years ago large tracts of woodland existed throughout the plains. Wildlife, specially blackbuck (*Antilope cervicapra*), chital (*Axis axis*), nilgai (*Boselaphus tragocamelus*), hyena (*Hyena hyena*), wolf (*Canis lupus*), fox (*Vulpes bengalensis*), jackal (*Canis lupus*) and porcupine (*Hystrix indica*), was also plentiful. Herds of blackbuck numbering several hundred individuals could be commonly seen in the vicinity of villages. However, conversion of woodlands into farmland and the easy availability of guns after Independence have almost completely decimated the blackbuck and chital, and considerably reduced the population of other species.

2. Occupational History

The occupational history of the region goes back to the late Middle Pleistocene. Stone tools and associated fossil faunal remains have been found in the alluvial deposit of the Yamuna near Kalpi in Orai district. Evidence is more plentiful from the terminal Pleistocene onwards when Upper Palaeolithic and later Mesolithic populations from the hilly country to the south of the Ganga river colonised the southeastern part of the plain. Their archaeological remains have been found at over 200 sites in the districts of Allahabad, Pratapgarh, Sultanpur, Jaunpur and Varanasi in the form of stone, bone and antler tools, ornaments, animal remains, structural features and large cemeteries (Kennedy 2000; Kennedy *et al*. 1986; Lukacs 1990.1992; V.D, Misra 1996, 2007: Pal 1992, 1994; Varma 1986 Sharma 1973; Sharma *et al*, 1980). The present distribution of hunter-gatherers, however, shows that their ancestors had spread all over the Indo-Gangetic plain in the remote past. Colonisation of the plain by farming communities seems to have begun, according to the recent radiocarbon dates from sites like Koldihwa, Jhusi and Hetapatti in Allahabad district, Tokwa in Mirzapur district, and Lahuradewa in Sant Kabir Nagar (formerly Basti) district in the fifth millennium B.C., and probably even earlier (Tewari *et al.* 2003, 2005), and was accelerated after the introduction of iron technology in the later half of the second millennium B.C. It is a remarkable phenomenon that, in spite of long and intensive occupation of this plain by rural and urban communities supported by agricultural economy, peoples adapted to a forest environment and hunting-foraging way of life have survived right into the twenty-first century.

3. Sources of Information

Incidental references to some hunting-gathering groups exist in ancient and medieval literature but these have not yet been properly searched. The modern accounts of these peoples date from the early nineteenth century, the earliest known to us being an article on the Badhiks and Thags by J. Shakespear (1818). It is, however, after 1860 that more accounts of these communities become available. These were written mainly by British administrators on the basis of information collected by themselves or through their subordinate British and Indian officials from members of the concerned communities. The main purpose behind collecting this information was to acquire comprehensive and accurate knowledge of the customs and habits of numerous Indian ethnic groups for their proper administration. This information is in the form of notes in decennial census reports, district gazetteers, articles in journals, and general ethnographic works

(Cline 1867; Leeds 1867; William 1869; Elliot 1869; Sherring 1872; Nesfield 1883; Plowden 1883; Meade 1886, 1905; Bhattacharya 1896; Risley 1901; Kirkpatrick 1911, 1913; Rose 1911; Ibbetson 1916; Blunt 1931; Turner 1933; Bonnington 1935). Most of the earlier accounts were subsequently synthesized by William Crooke in a comprehensive four-volume survey published in 1896 under the title *Tribes and Castes of the North-Western Provinces and Oudh*. This work, a veritable mine of anthropological information, gives brief ethnographic accounts, population figures, and distribution of all the communities of the upper and middle Ganga valley.

These accounts constitute our only source of information of these communities. J.C. Nesfield's article on the Kanjars published in 1883, for example, remains the most comprehensive chronicle of that community to this day. Although not always exhaustive and not prepared according to modern research methodology, these accounts nevertheless provide valuable insights into the dynamics of the cultural process by which the hunter-foragers managed to survive in a drastically altered natural and social environment by adding new economic pursuits to their traditional modes of adaptation and by forging links with peasant and urban societies.

4. Ethnic Groups

Although previous writers had described or mentioned a number of ethnic groups of the upper and middle Ganga valley, Crooke (1896 I: cvlvii-clix) was the first to prepare a comprehensive list of them. He listed a total of 215 communities and classified them into 61 groups on the basis of their occupations. The two groups which are of interest to us in the present context are: (1) 'Hunters, Fowlers, etc.'. and (2) 'Miscellaneous and Disreputable Livers'. Most of the communities in the group entitled 'Forest and Hill Tribes' also practise hunting-gathering in some degree but since they are confined mainly to the hilly tracts of Mirzapur district in the south and Himalayan hills in the north, they fall outside the scope of this chapter. A number of communities in several other groups also practise hunting-foraging and/or fishing, but they are not included here as hunting-gathering plays only a minor role in their subsistence.

In Crooke's list the communities included among 'Hunters and Fowlers' are: Aheriya, Baheliya, Bandi, Bangali, Gandhila, Gidiya and Kanjar, and those comprising 'Miscellaneous and Disreputable Livers' and practising some degree of hunting-foraging are: Badhik, Bawaria, Bhantu, Habura, Sansiya and Siyarmar. While communities in both groups practise hunting-foraging, those in the second group had acquired considerable notoriety for their indulgence in crime and/or prostitution by their women. As no information is available on Gidiya and Siyarmar, these are not included in the ensuing discussion.

To some extent the names of these communities, mostly derived from Sanskrit or Hindi (itself a language of Sanskrit origin) words and therefore obviously given by the other people, are themselves expressive of their economic status and overall lifestyle. Thus Aheriya is thought to be derived from 'Akhetaka' meaning 'hunter', Badhik from '*Vadhaka*' meaning a killer or murderer, Baheliya from '*Vyadha*' meaning 'one who pierces or wounds', 'a hunter', Kanjar from '*Kanan Char*', 'wanderer in the jungle', and Gandhila from '*Gandh*', meaning 'fetid' or 'malodorous'. The name Bawaria or Baori is believed to be derived from *Bawar* meaning a noose or snare which they use for trapping animals (Ibbetson 1916) or from *Banwar*, a creeper from which they make the noose or snare (Crooke 1896 I: 228). The Bawarias of western U.P. claim that the Gurjars call them Gidiyas and the Jats call them Baoris. Gidiya, according to Crooke, is merely a local name of the Bawarias.

Because there is considerable uniformity in the lifestyles of all these communities, most writers believe that not all of them may be distinct ethnic groups; instead they are more likely to be offshoots of one or more parental stocks who acquired separate names and identities by fission and geographical and cultural isolation. The Badhiks, for example, are believed by Crooke to be closely allied to the Bawarias and Baheliyas, are of mixed origin, and on the same grade as the Kanjars, Sansiyas, and similar vagrants. The Aheriyas, on the other hand, consider themselves to be identical with the Baheliyas, and both trace their ancestry to the poet-sage Valmiki. The Bangalis, according to Crooke, even though they disclaim any direct connection with Nats, Kanjars and similar vagrants, are obviously closely related to the latter. The Aheriyas of Aligarh admit that in former times, owing to the scarcity of women in the tribe, they used to introduce girls of other castes. This, they say, they have ceased to do in recent years, since the number of their females increased. In Aligarh they are known by different names, viz. Aheriya, Bhil or Karol. The Beriyas, in the opinion of Crooke (1896 I: 242-249), are closely allied with Sansiyas, Kanjars, Haburas, Bhantus, etc. They are a mixed race and many outcasts join them. The Haburas are very closely connected with Sansiyas and Bhantus and they have only recently become an endogamous group. The Sansiya, according to Crooke, is a near kinsman of the other degraded wandering races who occupy the same part of the country, such as the Kanjars, Beriyas, Haburas and Bhantus. Bhantus, again according to Crooke, are merely one branch of the Sansiya tribe, known elsewhere as Beriya, Habura or Kanjar. Some connect the derivation to the word Bhat (bard), as some Sansiyas act as bards or genealogists to some Rajputs and Jats. The Bhantus of Agra, Bareilly, Badaun, Moradabad, Ghazipur, Kheri and Sultanpur are said to follow the customs of the kindred tribes of Beriya, Habura and Sansiya.

5. Population and Distribution (Figs. 2-3)

The communities differ markedly in their numbers and geographical distribution. We have used data from 1891 and 1971 censuses to highlight changes that have taken place in these two parameters.

According to the 1891 census the largest population (33,754) was of the Baheliyas who were found in forty-three districts of the State, covering nearly the entire plain, though their concentration was more in the central and eastern districts. Numerically, the next were the Aheriyas (19,768) who were found only in sixteen, mainly western and central, districts. The third largest community were the Kanjars who, though numbering only 17,865, were the most ubiquitous, occurring in all the forty-seven plains districts, though relatively more numerous in the western and central parts. Of them Nesfield (1883: 369) says: 'There is scarcely a district in Upper India, in which small encampments of Kanjars cannot be seen at times, either in solitary jungle tracts which are favourable for game and secrecy, or in the outskirts of villages, wherever it may be convenient to them to halt and sell their wares'. The Beriyas, with a population of 15,313, were found in 36 districts, the major concentration being in

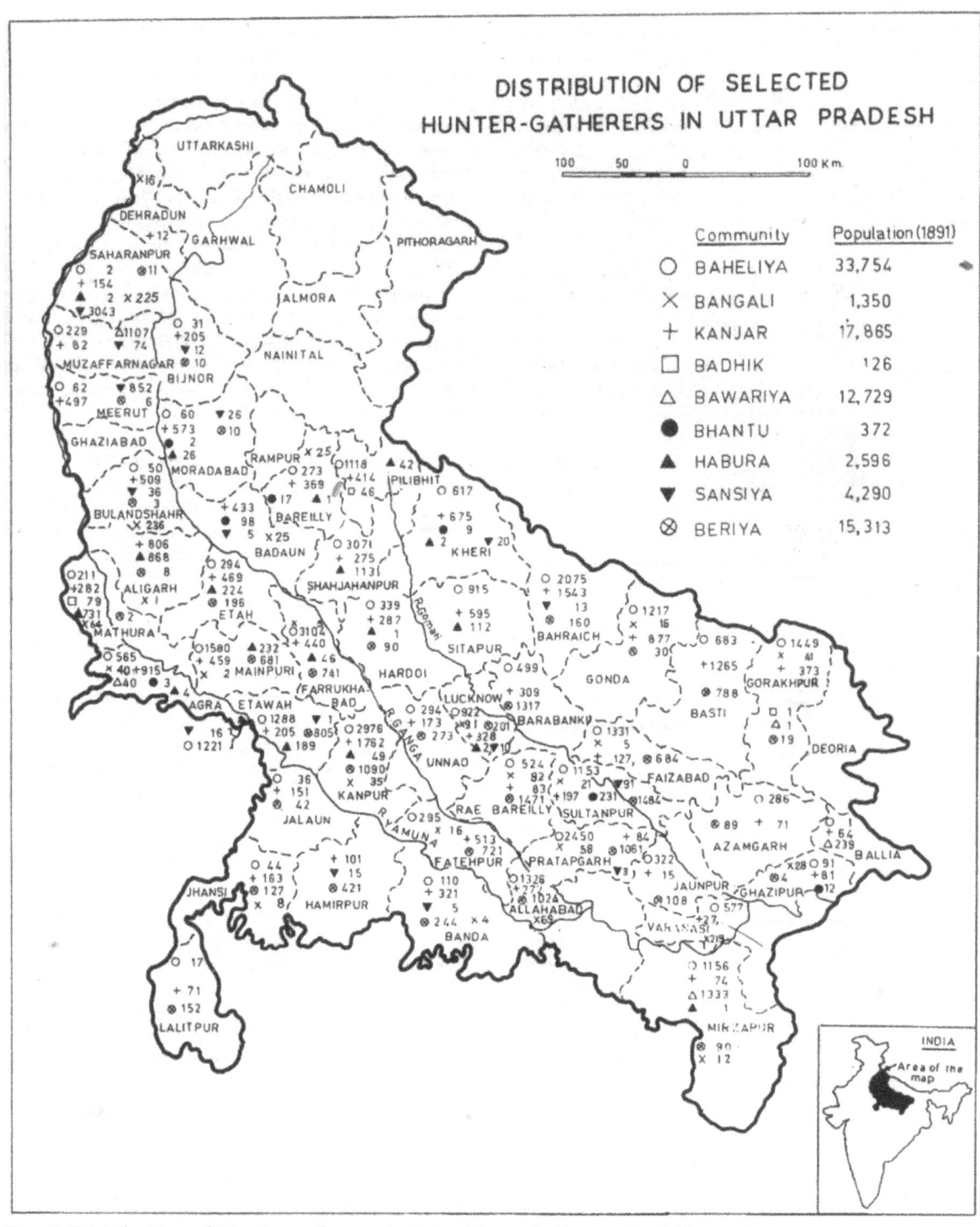

Fig. 2. Distribution of Hunter-gatherers in Uttar Pradesh (As per 1891 Census)

central and eastern districts. Next in sequence were the Sansiyas who numbered 4,290 persons and were spread over eighteen western and central districts, the majority being concentrated in Saharanpur and Meerut. The Bawarias and the Haburas had fairly similar populations, numbering 2,729 and 2,596 persons respectively. The former were found in six widely separated districts and the latter in seventeen western and central districts, being totally absent east and south of Lucknow. The Bangalis numbered only 1,350 and occurred in twenty-six districts from Dehradun in the

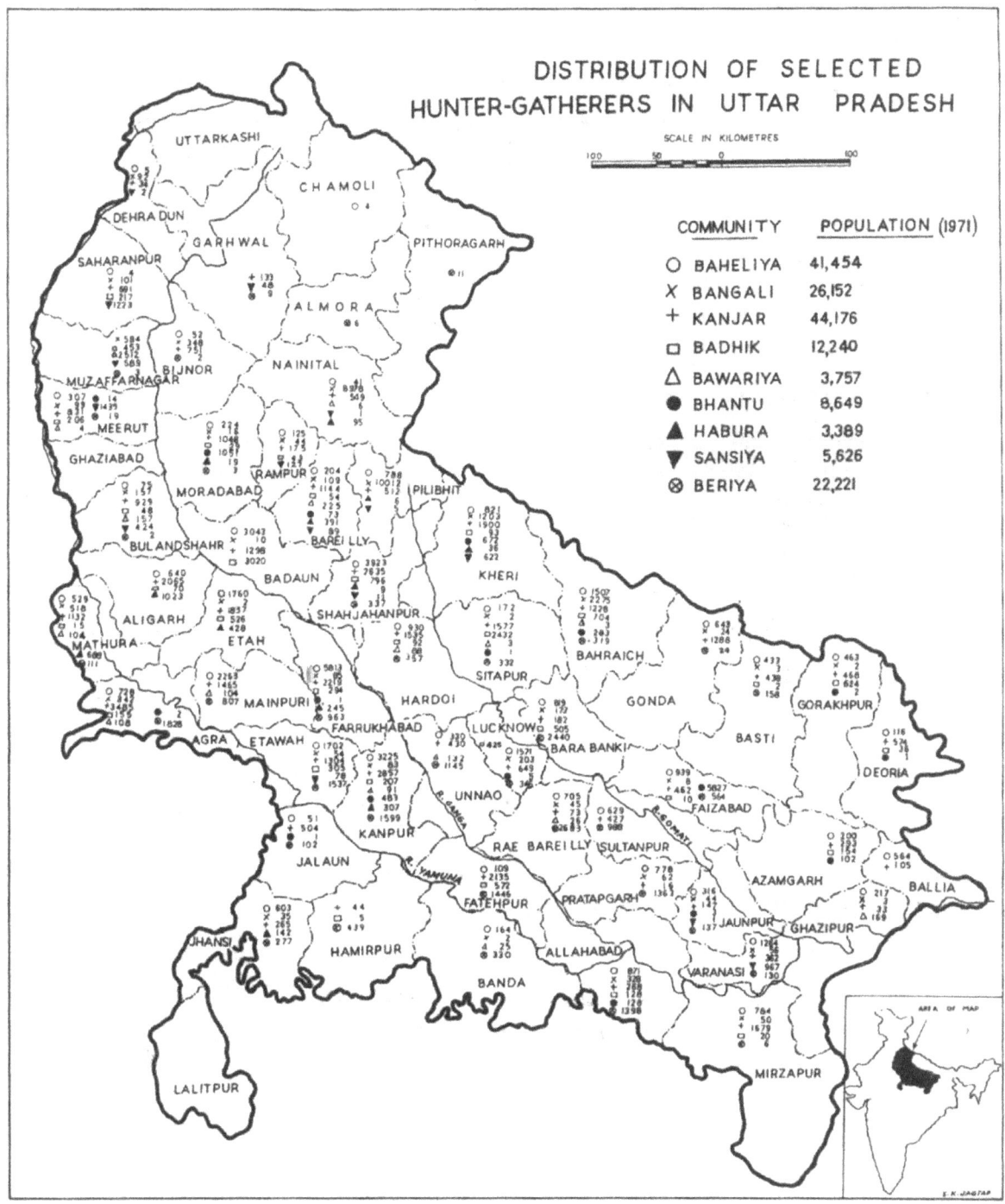

Fig. 3. Distribution of Hunter-gatherers in Uttar Pradesh (as per 1971 Census)

northwest to Gorakhpur in the southeast. The Bhantus, Bandis, Gandhilas, Badhiks and Gidiyas had restricted distributions. The Bhantus numbering 372 were confined to seven districts in the west and east, being totally absent in the centre of the State. The Gandhilas, with a population of 134, were confined to the two districts of Saharanpur and Muzaffarnagar. The Badhiks, numbering 126, occurred in Mathura and Pilibhit districts, with one individual recorded in Gorakhpur.

A comparison of the 1891 census population figures and distribution with those of the 1971 census shows that there have been very uneven increases in population over the period of eighty years.

While in some cases the increase has been less than fifty per cent, in others it has been 2000 per cent or even more. Thus, for example, the population of the Baheliyas rose from 33,754 to 41,454, that is by 22.8%. Similarly, the population of the Haburas rose from 2,596 to 3,389, that is by 30%, and that of the Sansiyas from 4,290 to 5,626, that is by 31%. Again, the increase in the case of the Bawarias was from 2,729 to 3,757, that is 37.7%. In the case of the Kanjars the increase was considerably higher, from 17,865 to 44,176, that is 147%. On the other hand, the increases in the case of the Bangalis, Bhantus and Badhiks were truly dramatic. The population of the Bangalis rose from 1,350 to 26,152, that is by 1837%, that of the Bhantus from just 372 to 8,649,. That is by 2225%, and that of the Badhiks from only 126 to 12,240, that is by 9614%. It is obvious that these very uneven increases have something to do with the methods of enumeration adopted by census workers.

The changes in the distribution pattern of the various communities have also been noteworthy though not as dramatic as those in the case of population. Only in the case of the Kanjars and the Beriyas there was no change at all; they continued to inhabit the 47 and 36 districts respectively in which they were present in 1891. The distribution of some communities increased, for example, of the Baheliyas from 43 to 47 districts, of the Bangalis from 26 to 36 districts, of the Badhiks from 3 to 31 districts, of the Bawarias from 6 to 16 districts, and of the Bhantus from 7 to 17 districts. There was a slight decline in the distribution area of two communities. The Sansiyas shrank from 18 to 15 districts, and the Haburas from 17 to 12 districts. The exact cause or causes of these changes can be ascertained only from a scrutiny of the data from intervening censuses and a study of the recent history of these communities.

6. Settlement Pattern

All these communities are described as vagrant and living their life in continuously shifting camps. Sections of some of them, however, appear to have settled temporarily or even permanently in the vicinity of villages and towns.

The Aheriyas, according to Sherring (1872 I: 405), are a tribe of wild and uncivilized people, exceedingly poor, and almost destitute of clothing. According to Crooke, the Bangalis wander all over the Upper Duab and Punjab and the Native States, and the Gandhilas wander about with little huts made of reed (*sirki*), seldom stay more than a few days in the same place, and call themselves indigenous to the Upper Ganges-Jumna Duab. Lieut. R.C. Temple (1882: 42) says about the Gandhilas that 'they are usually described in the courts as 'homeless sweepers'. They are `Musalmans of a very low order of intelligence, and in appearance more like beasts than men'. The Bhantus lead a nomadic life keeping as far as possible away from villages when they camp; men from different gangs would however combine in the event of a raiding expedition (Bonnington 1935: 37). The Beriyas also are vagrant, and those of them whose camps (*gol*) frequent the area around Nohkhera in Etah District meet at that place during the rainy season, and hold tribal council at which marriages and all matters affecting the caste are settled. The vagrant branch of the Sansiya tribe, according to Crooke, live under portable reed mats (*sirki*). They are very fond of dogs and keep a number of them to guard the camp. The camp is usually pitched on one of the high sandy ridges which are such a prominent feature in the landscape of the Upper Duab. They keep numerous bullocks and donkeys, which they use for transporting their huts and goods, as well as cows and goats for milk.

In the case of Kanjars, Nesfield (1883: 369) says 'All true Kanjars are addicted to a roving life; and if they halt for a time near some town or village, they put up their temporary sheds made with poles and matting, in a grove at some distance apart from the abodes of the settled inhabitants.... Their natural home is the forest'. The close association of the Kanjars with the forest is also exemplified by the custom of the girl's father giving away to his son-in-law as dowry 'a patch of forest assumed to be his own, which becomes thenceforth the property of the bridegroom, so long as the encampment remains near this place, or whenever it may return to it. No one without the bridegroom's consent will be authorised to use this piece of forest either for hunting or trapping, or for digging out the roots of *khaskhas*, or for gathering wild honey, or collecting medicinal herbs' (Nesfield 1883: 382-83). The practice of disposing of the dead body by exposure in the forest among several communities, like Kanjars and Baheliyas also shows that they preferred to live in the forest.

The exact size of the nomadic groups is not always mentioned but it appears to have been small. Kanjars, for example, according to Nesfield (1883: 370), 'are seldom or never seen in groups of more than 20 or 40 persons of all ages at a time, and the number is sometimes less. These little groups may unite sometimes for special and temporary objects. But large groups are never permanently formed There are some groups or clans, which make a habit of keeping within easy reach, while others seldom or never leave the forest. But even among the former, it is not merely the proximity of settled communities, which prevents the formation of larger groups. For even in the wider forest tracts, where there is ample space and no impediment from higher races, the same law of petty non-associative hordes prevails; and it would be a rare thing to find an encampment of more than, or even as many as 50 persons'. In the case of the Bhantus, a gang is said to be composed of a dozen families.

7. Subsistence

a. Hunting, Trapping and Fishing

All these groups lived in varying degrees by hunting and foraging, and most of them had few inhibitions about the choice of animal foods they ate, the only exception being beef which all of them avoided obviously in deference to the sentiments of their Hindu neighbours. The Aheriyas, according to Sherring (1872), catch snakes, roast, and eat them. This in fact is the chief employment of some of them. They are also to some extent fowlers. In Punjab they are said to catch and eat all kinds of wild animals. The occupation of the Baheliyas is described as hunting, bird trapping and collection of jungle produce. Bird catchers among them were known as 'Miskar', said to be a corruption of 'Mir Shikar' meaning 'head huntsman' or 'Maskar', meaning 'eater of meat'. One endogamous group among them is named Chiriyamar (bird killers), and the speciality of another group, named Karaul, is said to be stalking animals under cover of a tame ox used as a decoy. They have the reputation of being skilled *shikaris* (hunters) and game trackers. They eat the flesh of fowls, goat, deer and sheep, but not pork or beef, and they will not kill a cow, monkey and squirrel. They drink liquor freely. The Bandis, like the Baheliyas, are essentially bird catchers. The Bangalis eat the flesh of cloven or uncloven footed animals, fowls, all kinds of fish, and crocodiles. The Gandhilas eat squirrels, quails, tortoises, dogs, any kind of carrion, including putrid flesh, and vermin of all kinds which they catch.

The Kanjars, according to Nesfield, subsist by hunting jackals, foxes, wolves, hares, trapping birds and squirrels, and digging out snakes, mongooses, bandicoots, field rats, lizards, turtles and turtle eggs, and any other kind of vermin that chance may throw their way; all of which they eat indiscriminately. Whatever a Kanjar kills, from a wolf to a reptile, he eats; and most of what he finds dead, he eats also. He does not eat dogs nor monkeys.

The Badhiks eat game and vermin, such as foxes, jackals, and lizards. They believe that the use of jackal meat fortified them against the inclemencies of winter. According to Sherring, the Badhiks in some districts of U.P. are known as Khors or Siyar-Marwas (jackal-killers), on account of their habit of eating the flesh of the jackal. The Bawarias, like the Baheliyas and the Bandis, mainly live by catching birds of all kinds. They eat almost any kind of meat except beef, and indulge freely in liquor. For Bhantus, according to Wahi (1949), eating of certain quadrupeds like cow and deer is taboo. The Bhantu does not eat the creatures which live in water, like fish, turtle, etc. as they are considered dirty. The Haburas hunt and trap *goh* or iguana, *sanda* or monitor lizard, hedgehog, jackal, wild cat, buffalo, deer, fowls, tortoise, fish, crocodile, and other vermin. They eat all these and pork but not cow and donkey. The Beriyas, according to Crooke (1896 I: 243), eat whatever they can get, whether it be a rotten jackal or a piece of beef or mutton. They are seldom without large supplies of game and flesh of wild animals, of all kinds. A variety of birds they keep dried for medical purposes; mongooses, squirrels and flying foxes they eat with avidity as articles of luxury. Liquor and intoxicating drugs are indulged in to a large extent, and chief clans assume the title of Bhangi or drinkers of hemp (*bhang*) as a mark of honour. In the case of the Sansiyas the available accounts are silent regarding their hunting practices. But as they too are a nomadic people, camping in the forest and on sandy ridges, and are described as near kinsmen of the other wandering groups; it is almost certain that they too practise hunting in some measure.

b. Technology and Techniques of Hunting

Not much information is available in this regard except in the case of the Kanjars. The major tool and weapon of the Kanjars is the *khanti*. The name is probably derived from the Sanskrit *khan* meaning to dig or make a hole. The tool consists of a 1 m long wooden handle and an iron blade, about 30 cm long and sharpened into a curved point something like the blade of a knife and hafted at one end of the handle. The iron blade is procured by Kanjars from ironsmiths, and the handle is made by themselves. The implement serves as a dagger or short spear for killing wolves and jackals; as a tool for carving a secret entrance through the clay-wall of a villager's hut, where a burglary is meditated; as a spade or hoe for digging snakes, field rats, lizards, etc. out of their holes; for digging edible roots, and roots of *khaskhas* grass out of the earth, and as a hatchet for chopping wood. The *Khanti* or short spear is not merely used in close combat, but is thrown with almost unerring effect against wolves or jackals as they run.

In the use of their simple weapons, the Kanjars display extraordinary skill. The weapon with which they kill little birds is nothing but a pole pointed with a thin sharp spike or iron. The man lies motionless on a patch of ground, which he has first sprinkled with grain; and as the birds come hopping around him to pick up the grain, he fascinates one of them with the pole by giving it a serpent-like motion, and then spikes it through the body. Kanjars seldom or never use the bow and arrow; but they use the pellet bow, which requires much greater skill. The pellet is nothing but a little clay marble dried in the sun. With this they frequently shoot flying birds. For trapping a wolf in its lair they place a net and a light at one end of the hole, and commence digging at the other end. The wolf attracted by the light runs into the net, and the Kanjar then batters its head with a club and kills it.

The Baheliyas have a most ingenious mode of trapping birds with a series of thin bamboos, like a fishing rod, on which bird-lime (*lasa*) is smeared. This they push with great skill through the branches and leaves where a bird is sitting, and entangle his wings and feathers. According to Sherring (1872: 352), the Baheliya, while catching birds, is seated on the ground with a long pole in his hand, at one end of which is a sharp spike. He slowly introduces the pole among a number of birds carelessly hopping about picking up grain, giving it a zig-zag direction and imitating as much as possible the movement of snake. Having brought the point near one of the birds, which is fascinated by its stealthy approach, he suddenly jerks it into its breast, and then drawing it to him, releases the poor palpitating creature, putting it away in his bag, and recommences the same operation. The Baheliyas also catch birds with a kind of lime taken from the *Maddar* tree, by means of a long pole, as in the former instance. The viscous substance at the end of the pole, on touching the bird, sticks to it, and it is caught. As for the use of bow and arrows, it is mentioned only in the case of the Beriyas who are also said to be great adepts in laying snares and traps (Crooke 1896 I: 243).

c. Gathering

All these communities also exploited wild plant foods for their subsistence though information on this aspect of their economy is not as plentiful as on hunting. The Aheriyas collect gum of the *dhak* or (*palas*) (*Butea frondosa*) and acacia trees, and honey. Bawaria women sell the roots and herbs, etc. which they collect in the jungles. The Kanjars gather 'such roots and vegetable products as require no cultivation, and extract juice from the palm tree, which, after it has become fermented, is a favourite beverage of almost all the wandering and low caste tribes of India' (Nesfield 1883: 369). They were, and are to this day, expert honey collectors.

8. Other Occupations

All these communities also engage in collecting a wide range of forest produce which they use to make a variety of articles for the needs of the village and town people. These are either bartered or sold. The Aheriyas collect leaves of *palas* for making platters which they sell to Hindus. They also collect reeds for making baskets, etc. The Baheliyas too collected jungle produce, made ropes, and were employed as watchmen and in other services. In Mirzapur some of them worked in lac factories, and a few cultivated as non-occupancy tenants. The Gandhilas collect grass and straw for making baskets and sieves, catch quails, clean and sharpen knives and swords, cut wood, and generally do odd jobs (Rose 1919 II: 278). Bawaria women are also experts in making patchwork quilts which they sell. The Beriya male practises 'everything that enables him to pass an easy life without submitting to any law of civilized government or the amenities of social life. His women deal with palmistry, cupping with buffalo horns, administering moxas and drugs for spleen and rheumatism. They are also tattooers. At home the women make mats of palm leaves, while the husbands cook' (Crooke 1896 I: 243).

The Kanjars practise a variety of crafts, the products of which they sell to village and town people in exchange for grain, milk, pigs, etc. They make mats of *sirki* or *munj* (*Saccrum munja*) reeds, baskets of cane, fans of palm leaves, and rattles of plaited straw, the last sold to Hindu children as toys. From the stalks of *munj* grass and from the roots of *palas* tree they make ropes. They prepare the skins for drums which are sold to Hindu musicians. They make plates and cups of *palas* leaves for selling to sweetmeat makers. The mats of *sirki* reeds with which they cover their own temporary sheds, are largely used by cart drivers to protect their goods and themselves against rain. The toddy or juice of the palm tree which they extract and ferment, partly for their own use, finds a ready sale among low caste Hindus. Kanjars are the chief stone-cutters in north India, specially in the manufacture of grinding stone which is used in every rural home. They gather the white wool-like fibre which grows in the pods of the *salmali* or silk cotton tree and twist it into thread for the use of weavers. They have an almost complete monopoly in the manufacture of brushes for cleaning cotton yarn and in the collection and sale of *khaskhas* grass for making screens that are widely used as room coolers during summer months (Nesfield 1883).

The eastern Bawarias are now settled and cultivate land as tenants. The Aheriyas in some places, as in the Aligarh district, are also beginning to cultivate land and are becoming more civilized day by day. Besides, the Bangalis, Kanjars and Beriyas all acted as rustic surgeons for bleeding and cupping. The Gandhilas and the Beriyas engage their women in prostitution, and both beg and eat the leavings of upper caste Hindus. Bandis are drummers and bird-catchers in the Himalayan *Tarai.* Their chief business is catching birds for sale. They also make a living by catching birds and bringing them into cities where pious people, such as Jain Baniyas, pay them to release a bird as an act of piety or as a charm to take away disease from a sick person. In their habits and occupation they resemble the Baheliyas. Bawarias, who are also bird-catchers, sell the birds that are eatable; others they take to the houses of rich Jain merchants and make an income by releasing them from their cages.

9. Crime

Detailed information is available about the criminal activities of these communities. Except the Baheliyas, Bandis and Bangalis all the other groups indulged in crime though the degree of their addiction varied.

The Aheriyas, according to Crooke, chiefly carry on the business of burglary and highway robbery, and they are about the most active and determined criminals in the Province. Their children learn to steal at an early age and by about sixteen years are ready to join in the expeditions. Gangs consist of from ten to twenty people though the number may occasionally go up to forty. Their leaders (*Jamadars*) are elected for their skill, intelligence, and daring. When questioned about their identity while on a raiding expedition they generally give the name of a respectable community. They avoid putting up at *sarais* (inns) and generally encamp 100 or 200 paces from the high road to watch travellers, carts, and vans passing. They all carry bludgeons, but one or two in the gang may also carry a sword. They commence by pelting the guards of the carts or camels with pieces of limestone (*kankar*) or stone. This generally causes them to flee; but, if not, they assemble and threaten them with their bludgeons. They claim that even though they were always thieves by profession, they did not take to highway robbery till the great famine of 1833, and they were taught this easy mode of living by the Baheliyas.

The Gandhilas, according to Major Temple, are inveterate thieves, especially of dogs, which they eat. The Kanjars are essentially hunters rather than criminals, but a few of them are known to engage in robberies. According to Nesfield, many of the *dakaits*, or gang-robbers, who infest the public highways at night, are Kanjars; and in the pursuit of this calling they are sometimes associated with evil-doers from among the Hindu community.

The Badhiks were known to be notorious *dakaits* (highway robbers). One of their specialities used to be disguising themselves as Brahmans and Bairagis (mendicants) and associating with pilgrims returning from the Ganges, for whom they used to perform mock religious ceremonies, and then stupefy them with *datura* (thorn apple) and rob them. They were in the habit of making plundering expeditions. Sherring (1872: 390) describes them as a caste of professional robbers and assassins.

The Bawarias, according to Crooke, were traditional killers and plunderers for the princes, and they never had occasion to labour at tillage. The western Bawarias are best known as a criminal tribe. When they go on their predatory excursions which extend over a large part of Northern India, they change their appearance by putting on the dress of faqir (mendicant). The only way of finding them out is by a peculiar necklace of small wooden beads, which they all wear, and by a kind of gold pin which they wear fixed to their front teeth. The peculiarity about their thieving is that when they enter a house they take with them some dry grain, which they throw about in the dark, so as to be able by the rattle to ascertain the position of brass or other metal objects. In the early 1980s a gang of Bawarias had stolen jewellery worth several lakh rupees from a temple in Jabalpur. They were caught, tried in a court of law and sentenced to imprisonment. The case, because of the daring nature of the crime, received wide publicity in the press and the M.P. Police even brought out a booklet on this case. The community continues to be active in crime right till today. As late as 13 October, 2007 the TV News channel *Aaj Tak* reported that nine Bawarias were arrested by the police in the Sarojini Nagar locality of Lucknow.

The Bhantus have been known to travel very great distances in disguise for the purpose of committing thefts, robberies and dacoities. The gang usually consists of some 30 to 40 people. Often cruel and violent methods were adopted to compel the victims to reveal the hidden places of their treasure, such as forcing women to sit on burning charcoal, or raping, etc. The traditional weapon of attack was a short hard stick, thrown with tremendous force. In more recent years, however, guns have been adopted. Many of their gangs are led by women. It is also apparently legitimate for a Bhantu woman to use her womanly wiles in the advancement of the tribe's criminal activities (Bonnington 1935). According to Wahi (1949), for the Bhantu committing a crime for the tribe is like a religious injunction and hence a social virtue. The more efficient a Bhantu is in committing crime, the higher is his status in his society. The young girls refuse to accept as bridegrooms any but the adept criminals. Children are trained to commit crimes. They are taught everything regarding disguise, use of code words, hiding small ornaments, rings, etc. in their throats.

In the case of the Beriya, his women loaf about villages and procure information about valuable property for their male relations. The males will steal crops from fields and property from the houses of the villagers. They have also been known to commit more serious crimes and attack camel carts and wedding parties at night (Crooke 1896 I: 247).

The vagrant branch of Haburas are said to be the pest of the neighbourhoods and are continually robbing standing crops, attacking carts and passengers along the roads, committing robberies and even *dakaities*. The boys are trained at first on field robbery, and are then taken out on excursions for the purpose of burglary. When they go to rob fields, the gang consists of not less than twenty people, and for the purpose of burglary eight or nine together. They never carry any weapons but bludgeons; they seldom use violence (Crooke 1896 II: 479-80).

The Sansiyas are one of the most audacious criminal tribes in the Province. In the Upper Duab they had no other means of livelihood except *dakaiti* (dacoity), road robbery, thefts from vehicles, barns, and from persons sleeping in the fields. In the course of their operations, unlike the Haburas or Beriyas, they were always ready to commit violence, and have been known to cause serious bodily injury and even death with the heavy bludgeons which in recent years they had substituted for short clubs. During highway robbery they suddenly attack passengers or the drivers of vehicles with showers of stones. If this failed to compel them to abandon their property, they fall on them with their bludgeons. Another device was to disguise themselves as constables, and in the course of a mock search to rob travellers. They do not stay at *sarais* but encamp outside a village or town, and being well dressed, pretend to be Banjaras (merchants). In Aligarh they are divided into seven gangs (*gol*), of which leaders of five were women and two were led by men. The reason that women so often command the gangs is because so many of the males are habitually in jail (Crooke 1896 IV: 283-84).

10. Attitude of the Government

Until the advent of the British the tribal societies enjoyed relative freedom from interference in their affairs by the ruling elite. During the decay of the Moghul empire in the eighteenth and early nineteenth centuries there was a general decline of law and order. Gangs of Thugs, Pindarees and other criminal groups roamed around freely plundering travellers and traders. Some of these hunter-gatherer groups living in this environment of lawlessness and probably already accustomed to crime took to it on a larger scale. When the British established their rule in the Ganga plains, they took various measures to suppress these criminal groups. As a part of this process in 1871 the government passed the Criminal Tribes Act. Under this Act the government could declare any tribe or group as a Criminal Tribe provided adequate evidence existed for doing so. Steps were also taken for settling these vagrant people and keeping a surveillance on them. This Act was amended several times (1897, 1911, 1923, and 1924) to remove the various lacunae and make it more effective. Under this Act provisions were made, among other things, for (i) local governments to declare a tribe as a Criminal Tribe without inquiring its settlements or the provision of the means of living; (ii) registration of the members of the tribes and taking of their finger impressions for observation and supervision; (iii) separation of the children of habitual offenders from their parents and putting them in reformatory 'settlements'; and (iv) restricting the more criminally minded members of the notified tribe to any specified area or interning them in settlements to be specially established for them. Under this Act a total of 115 communities all over the country were declared as Criminal Tribes. Among the twelve communities discussed in this chapter all except Bandi were included in this category.

In pursuance of this policy the British government established a number of settlements for criminal tribes. A strict watch was kept on the movements of the inmates of the settlements, and jobs were provided to them to wean them away from crime. This policy succeeded in large measure in reforming the criminal groups.

The Indian government soon after Independence in 1947 felt that it was unfair to condemn whole communities or groups as Criminal Tribes for crimes committed only by a section of them. Accordingly, the government appointed a committee in 1949 to enquire into the working of the Criminal Tribes Act, 1924, and to make recommendations for its modification or repeal. 'The Criminal Tribes Act Enquiry Committee' in its report recommended the repeal of the Act. The Indian Parliament passed the Criminal Tribes Law (Repeal) Act, 1952. By this law all the Criminal Tribes were declared denotified (Majumdar 1941-42; Saksena 1975).

In the Constitution of India which came into effect in 1950 special provisions were made for the speedy development of the untouchable castes of the Hindu society and the tribal peoples. These two classes were categorised as Scheduled Castes and Scheduled Tribes, respectively. Their names were specified by Presidential Orders first issued in 1950 and amended on subsequent occasions. In these orders none of the groups discussed in this chapter were included among the Scheduled Tribes. However, except Aheriya, Bandi and Gandhila all of them were included among the Scheduled Castes. From 1951 onwards the Census Department stopped enumerating communities on caste basis. However, the population of the Scheduled Castes and Scheduled Tribes continued to be separately enumerated. As a result we do not have data even on the population and distribution of those denotified communities which were not included under Scheduled Castes. But for a few exceptions (Gautam 1983; Majumdar 1941-42, 1944, 1947; Mahalanobis *et al.* 1946; Wahi 1949; Saksena 1975) little research has been conducted in recent decades on the condition of the various denotified communities, and so we have virtually no information on the present condition of these hunter-gatherer / criminal tribes.

11. Interaction with the Larger Society

There is no evidence to suggest that any of these hunter-gatherer groups have entered the Ganga plains in historically recorded times, i.e. during the last two-and-half thousand years or so. On the contrary, there are ample references in the early Sanskrit literature to show that the Aryan colonisers of the plains in the second and first millennia B.C. encountered indigenous dark-coloured populations whom they called Nishadas and Shudras. On the other hand, the extensive presence of Mesolithic populations in the southeastern part of the plain would strongly suggest that the living hunter-gatherers are descendants of those populations. In this context it is to be noted that the anthropological study of the human skeletons recovered from the sites of Sarai Nahar Rai, Mahadaha and Damdama in the Pratapgarh district of Uttar Pradesh shows that "these skeletons are impressive in appearance – large, heavily muscled, tall, and hyperrobust people who appear to have attained their full ontogenetic potential in a demanding hunting-foraging lifeway. When viewing photographs of these Gangetic hominids, the late Kenneth P. Oakley was moved to remark, "They look like European Cro-Magnon skeletons!" (Kennedy 2000: 226). Although we are not aware of any anthropometric study of the hunting-gathering peoples discussed in this chapter, from our own encounters with them we know that they are tall, well-built and sturdy, and look very different from the usually short, dark-complexioned, and snub-nosed people of many of the lower castes in the Ganga plains. This physical similarity between the hunter-gatherers and the Mesolithic people strongly suggests that the former are biologically descended from the latter.

Agriculture-based settled societies began to appear in the plains at the beginning of the fifth millennium B.C., and colonisation of the plain by them was intensified after the introduction of iron technology toward the end of the second millennium B.C. The social ideology of the economically and politically dominant Aryan society was shaped by Brahmanism, the forerunner of present-day Hinduism. From the middle of the first millennium B.C. this society became increasingly organised into the caste system. This system was hierarchical, and the place of every community in it was determined by its occupation, food habits, political power, and the degree to which it followed Brahmanical rituals. No social group which had any economic or political interaction with Aryan society could remain unaffected by the caste system.

The hunter-gatherers living in the Ganga plains shared their environment with the caste communities living in villages and towns. Being economically, technologically and politically weaker than the Hindu caste groups, they could be easily dominated by the latter. Their labour was useful for expanding agriculture and settlement, and their traditional craft skills in rope making, wood working, basket weaving, etc. could be utilized for producing articles required by the peasantry. Thus many autochthonous peoples were slowly drawn into the Aryan caste-based society. The place they got in the hierarchical system depended on their qualifications stated above. Those who continued to live in the forest away from permanent settlements managed to retain their economic, social, religious and political freedom. But as population grew and more and more forest was cleared, the habitat of the hunter-gatherers continued to shrink, and all of them were obliged to come into contact with the dominant caste groups. This situation was reached long before the British established their control over the Ganga plains in the nineteenth century. The steadily increasing contact between the Aryan settlers and the largely nomadic indigenous populations was bound to influence the social and religious ideologies of both the societies. And this is what we find when we examine their institutions.

The hunger-gatherers had their distinctive religious and social beliefs and practices. While they have retained these, they have also adopted some of the Hindu deities and rituals. More than that, even while retaining their identity as tribes they have not remained unaffected by the philosophy of caste. They have accepted, even if reluctantly, their own low position in relation to upper Hindu castes, and imbibed the Hindu attitudes towards various castes in their dealings with them. On the other hand, large sections of the hunter-gatherers have been fully incorporated into the caste system and have totally lost their identity as distinct non-Hindu indigenous peoples. The Hindu society, in turn, has absorbed some of the religious beliefs and practices of the hunter-gatherers, specially at the level of the lower castes, but also to some extent at the level of upper castes as well.

The religion of the indigenous peoples as we know it from the ethnographic accounts is mainly centred around the worship of ancestors and local gods and goddesses. Nesfield's description of the religion of the Kanjars as being 'without idols, without temples, and without a priesthood' is in its essence true of the religion of all the other communities discussed in this chapter. The aborigines live in constant dread of the evil spirits, the souls of the departed, who are said to enter into the bodies of the living as a punishment for past misdeeds or neglect of burial rites, and to produce most of the ills. All deaths, but those caused by natural decay or by violence, are ascribed to the agency of evil spirits. The ancestors as also the other deities are periodically propitiated by the offering of animal sacrifices to prevent them from causing any harm in the form of injury, sickness, and death (Nesfield 1883).

The special deity of the Badhiks, Bawarias and Bhantus is the goddess Kali, to whom they offer goats. Aheriyas and Sansiyas worship Devi (mother goddess). The goddesses of the Beriyas are Devi, Kali, and Jwalamukhi. In Bijnor the Beriyas usually worship Kali Bhawani. In Mathura they have a local goddess, Kela Devi, to whom on special occasions they sacrifice a buffalo or goat. The Kanjars worship at least three goddesses. These are *Mata* (mother), the small pox goddess, and *Masani*, the spirit of the burning ground. In addition, these communities also have some gods. The clan gods of the Baheliyas of the eastern districts are Kalu Bir and Parihar. To Kalu Bir a young pig is offered and wine poured on the ground. Parihar receives a sacrifice of fowls and cakes. In Oudh a goat is sacrificed to Kale Deo. The chief god of the Kanjars is Mana. He is worshipped with the sacrifice of a pig or goat, or sheep, or fowl, and an offering of roasted flesh and liquor. Mekhasur (ram demon) is the tribal godling of the Aheriyas for whom they make a house shrine in a room set apart for the purpose.

While continuing the worship of their own deities, these communities have also taken to the worship of some deities of the Hindu pantheon, as also of animals, plants and rivers which the Hindus hold sacred. They have also adopted some of the Hindu festivals. Thus the Gandhilas and Haburas worship Parmeshwar, the supreme Hindu God. The Sansiyas believe in great God, i.e. Bhagwan or Parmeshwar or Narayan. Like the Hindus, the Baheliyas hold the Ganga sacred and swear by her. The Beriyas bathe in the Ganga in the honour of their dead. When they take oath they turn to the river and swear by mother Ganga. The Bhantus also offer *arghya* (water) to *pipal* tree and have a special worship of the *aonla* (*Phyllanthus emblica*) on the eleventh of the bright half of the month of *Phalgun*. For Nagapanchami festival their women draw pictures of snakes on the walls of their houses and throw milk over them. Men take milk to the jungle and place it before the hole of a snake. Their chief oath is either on the Ganga or stand under a *pipal* tree or hold a leaf of it in the hand. The Beriyas also celebrate the usual holidays Salono, Holi, Diwali and Dasahra. Most of the festivals of the Aheriyas are those common to all Hindus.

Some members of these hunting-gathering communities have also started using the services of Brahmin priests in their ceremonies and rituals. Among the Baheliyas the ordinary low village Brahmins act as their priests at domestic ceremonies. All the Haburas call themselves Hindus though they accept little or no service from Brahmins. The Beriyas employ Brahmins only for giving omens at marriages, and it is only the very lowest Brahmins who serve them. Among the Aheriyas a match is arranged with the help of a Brahmin and a barber.

Due to contact with the Muslims these aborigines have adopted the worship of a number of Muslim saints. Thus the Bawarias worship Zahir Diwan, and the Aheriyas worship Panch Pir's shrine near Aligarh. The offerings at the shrine are taken by a Muslim. The Aheriyas also worship Miyan Sahib and Jakhiya. Many of the Beriyas worship Sayyid which they understand to represent Muhammad, the prophet. The Bhantus also worship Sayyid. The Sansiyas have a belief in a godling known as Miyan, who may be Ghazi Miyan or the saint of Amroha and Jalesar. The Beriya is either Hindu or Musalman according to the population he lives in. Some are Kabirpanthis or Sikhs, some disguise themselves as Jogis, Faqir, etc.

Even while not fully integrated into the caste structure of the Hindu society these aboriginal groups have to a certain extent imbibed the ideology of caste, and they observe some of the taboos with regard to food and drink in their dealings with other kindred groups as well as caste societies. Thus the Baheliyas will not touch a Bhangi, Dom and Dhobi. The Aheriyas will eat *kachchi* (cereal food cooked in water) only from the Ahirs, Barhis, Jats and Kahars; they eat *pakki* (cereal food cooked by frying in *ghee* or oil) from a Nai. No other caste will eat with the Gandhilas, but some of them eat food from the hands of Kanjars, Sansiyas and similar vagrants. Among the Sansiyas those who are beginning to settle down claim, however, a much greater degree of purity and pretend not to eat *kachchi* except from high castes. The Haburas in Aligarh will not take food from four castes, namely Chamar, Dhobi, Bhangi and Kalar. In Bijnor they will drink from the hands of all Hindus except Chamars, Bhangis, Kanjars, Sansiyas and the like. In Bijnor, Mathura and other places they will eat the leavings of all high caste Hindus. The Haburas who have settled down to agriculture and become fairly respectable members of society are gradually shedding the filthy habits and customs of their vagrant life under the influence of Hindus. As they become more acculturated, they trace their pedigree to the Rajputs. In Etah it is reported that if a member of the tribe commits any theft or an immoral act, he is excommunicated for a certain time and is not admitted until he has drawn blood from some part of his body, usually the nose.

The impact of Hinduism is particularly evident on the methods of disposal of the dead among these communities. Their traditional method of disposing of the dead was by burial or exposure or submersion in water whereas among the Hindus it is invariably by cremation except in very special cases. But slowly the aborigines are giving up other methods in favour of cremation. The Kanjars use three different modes to dispose of their dead; submersion in deep water by fastening a stone to the corpse; cremation; and burial. The first method is the least common; the last is the one most frequently practised as well as the most highly esteemed. The method of cremation, Nesfield thinks, may have been borrowed from the Hindus. The Bawarias burn the adult dead and bury the unmarried people. Among the Aheriyas the rich people cremate the dead; poorer people bury, or consign the corpse to some river. After cremation the ashes are usually taken to the Ganga, but some people leave them at the pyre.

The Beriyas and Haburas are described as being in the intermediate stage between burial and cremation. The Beriyas of Farrukhabad touch the left foot of the corpse with fire and then bury it. In Etawah they cremate the dead and collect the ashes, which they put into an earthen pot, and then bury this in the ground, raising over it a small earthen platform. The Haburas in Mathura either cremate and leave the ashes where the corpse was burnt, or throw the corpse into the Jamuna. In Bijnor they either bury or expose the corpse in the jungle. In Aligarh, when they are well off, they cremate the dead. From Etah it is reported that when a man dies at home he is cremated, the bones are buried on the spot, and a masonry platform erected over them. If a man dies at a distance from home, his bones are brought to one of the regular camping places of the tribe, and are there buried.

The real vagrant Sansiyas often merely expose their dead in the jungle. In Aligarh the Chanduwala Sansiyas cremate the dead; with the others burial is the rule. In Mirzapur they bury the dead. Bhantus of all *gotras* (clans), except that of Dholiya, cremate their dead.

12. Assimilation into the Caste System

Large sections of these hunter-gatherers have been completely assimilated into the Hindu society over the millennia. But they were largely relegated to the lowest position (of untouchables) in the caste hierarchy because of their economic position (hunting-gathering), their food habits (eating wild animals despised by the Hindus, and consuming liquor), general poverty, ignorance of Brahmanical ritual, and lack of political power. In the case of the Aheriyas, for example, Sir H. M. Elliot describes them as a branch of the Dhanuks from whom they are distinguished by not eating dead carcasses, as the Dhanuks do. The Dhanuks are an untouchable Hindu caste who are now completely settled. They live by keeping swine and settle on the fringe of villages. Their women work as midwives even for the Brahmins. The communities with less obnoxious food habits and possessing craft skills useful to the Hindu society were given higher status. This is the only way in which the existence of the large number of artisan, service, and untouchable castes in the Ganga plains can be explained.

13. Conclusion

Hunter-gatherer communities have lived in the Ganga plains from at least the Mesolithic period (c. 8,000 B.C.), and probably earlier. With the introduction of agricultural economy from fifth millennium B.C. onwards village and urban centres grew up steadily. As a consequence the habitat of the hunter-gatherers was modified with increasing intensity. From then on they had to share their environment with peasant, pastoral, and trading communities, and were drawn into exchange systems and market economy. In response to the changes in their natural and social environment they rescheduled their traditional economic strategies by orienting their technical skills for providing goods and services to the village and urban populations. These goods included honey, meat of wild game, minor forest produce, hides for drums, baskets, winnowing fans, palm leaf fans, ropes, weavers' brushes, mats, leaf platters and cups, screens of *khaskhas* grass, thread of cotton tree fibre, and grinding and milling stones. The services they usually rendered were acting as medicinemen and surgeons, suppliers of herbal drugs and perfumes, entertainers, and herders of buffaloes and camels. Some groups like the Aheriya, Baheliya, Sansiya and Habura became professional thieves and robbers while continuing their traditional economic behaviour.

Economic interaction with Hindu society naturally brought them under the influence of the caste system. Sections of these communities were completely assimilated into this hierarchical system and were assigned a social ranking in conformity with the professional services they rendered, and their lifeways, specially their food habits. Others who continued to persist with their traditional modes of living remained on the periphery of Hindu society. However, the acculturation of these groups into the larger society has been an ongoing process, and it has been considerably accentuated by the increase in the pace of economic and social development after Independence. In their turn, these communities have been trying to improve their status in the caste system by tracing their ancestry to Hindu folk heroes and by adopting Brahmanical rituals and food habits. Their categorisation as Scheduled Castes by the government hinders this effort even while it entitles them to preferential treatment in educational and employment opportunities (Misra and Nagar 1989; Nagar and Misra 1990). As the Kanjars are the best studied of these hunter-gatherers, we describe them in more detail in the ensuing chapter.

THE KANJARS

1. Introduction

Archaeologists have been using ethnographic analogies from present-day simple societies to interpret archaeological data and reconstruct past patterns of life from the earliest days of prehistoric studies (Sollas 1924). In the early days the ethnographic data used by them was derived from the studies conducted by social anthropologists. The interests of social anthropologists were mainly concentrated on social and religious institutions and customs and they took only a marginal interest in the economic organisation, technology and material culture of these societies. Archaeologists are, however, more interested in these latter aspects of primitive societies. During the past five decades or so there has been considerable renewal of interest among archaeologists in general, and prehistorians in particular, in the value of ethnographic analogies. Many prehistorians are now themselves conducting ethnographic studies among the few surviving hunter-gatherer communities to understand their adaptive patterns and to use that knowledge for the interpretation of archaeological data of past hunter-gatherer (Palaeolithic and Mesolithic) societies. The publication of the proceedings of the symposium *Man the Hunter* (Lee and DeVore 1968) gave a great impetus to such studies. Among the more notable studies in this field are those by J.P. White (1967), R.B. Lee (1979), Richard Gould (1969, 1980), L.R. Binford (1978) and J.E. Yellen (1977).

In India a number of hunting-gathering communities still exist and many more existed in the recent past. Some of them like the Birhors (Roy 1925), Chenchus (Furer-Haimendorf 1943), and Kadars (Ehrenfels 1952; Luiz 1962) have been studied in some detail by social anthropologists. Valuable data has been collected, for example, on the Yanadis, Yerukulas and Chenchus by M.L.K. Murty (1981a, 1981b), on the Phase Pardhis by K.C. Malhotra and associates (Malhotra et al. 1983), on the Boyas by M.S. Nagaraja Rao (Nagaraja Rao and Malhotra 1965), on the Yanadis by J.S. Jayaraj (1984) and D.R. Raju (1988), on the Gonds and other tribes of central India by Malti Nagar (1982, 1983, 1985), on the Parjas and other groups in Orissa by S.C. Nanda (1985); on the Kurukhs by Zarine Cooper (1997); on the Van Vagris by V.N. Misra (1990), on the Bhils, Kalbeliyas, Pardhis by V.N. Misra and Malti Nagar (Misra 2007; Nagar and Misra 1993, 1994) and on the Kols, Musahars and Mallahs by Shahida Ansari (2000, 2001, 2005). However, detailed monographic studies of hunter-foragers from an archaeological perspective are few and far between.

The popular impression is that hunting-gathering communities in India are mainly confined to the hilly and forested regions of the country, like the Aravalli, Vindhya and Satpura Hills, Western and Eastern Ghats, Chota Nagpur Plateau, and northeast India outside the Bramhaputra Valley. As the topography of these regions rendered them unsuitable for large-scale irrigation-based agriculture and for smooth transport and communication, they did not attract advanced agriculturists until the pressure of population in the more favourable alluvial plains forced farming groups to move into these less attractive environments in search of arable land. The hunter-foragers and shifting cultivators could therefore continue their way of life and retain their cultural identity for much longer than in the large alluvial plains.

However, it is not widely known that even in the alluvial plains of north India which began to be colonised by settled farming-based communities more than 5,000 years ago and which are among the most densely populated regions of the country today, a number of communities living at least partly by hunting and gathering have survived right into the twenty-first century. In the plains of Uttar Pradesh (U.P.) some of these groups are: the Aheriya, Badhik, Baheliya, Bandi, Bangali, Bawaria, Beria, Bhantu, Gandhila, Habura, Kanjar, Kol, Musahar, and Sansiya. A knowledge of the way of life of these societies can be an invaluable source of information to archaeologists for reconstructing the cultures of the prehistoric hunter-gatherers as well as for understanding the dynamics of the process by which the hunter-foragers managed to survive in a drastically altered natural and social environment.

Unfortunately, little research is being done on these communities today, either by archaeologists or even by anthropologists. In the meantime their way of life is fast undergoing change as with the loss of their natural habitat they can no longer pursue their traditional lifestyles. Obliged to coexist with more advanced rural and urban people they have had to readjust their traditional adaptive strategies by taking to new occupations and forging new social relationships with other communities.

However, valuable data on them was collected by British administrators in the later part of the nineteenth and early part of the twentieth century. The main purpose behind collecting this information was to acquire comprehensive and accurate knowledge of the customs and habits of numerous Indian ethnic groups to help in their proper administration. This information is in the form of notes in decennial census reports, district gazetteers, articles in journals, and general ethnographic works. Most of the earlier accounts were subsequently synthesized by William Crooke in a comprehensive four volume ethnographic survey published in 1896 under the title *Tribes and Castes of the North-Western Provinces and Oudh*. This work, a veritable mine of anthropological information, gives brief ethnographic accounts, population figures, and the distribution of all these communities of the upper and middle Ganga valley.

One of the most widely distributed hunting-gathering communities of north India are the Kanjars, and this chapter is devoted to an account of their life.

2. Environmental Setting

Although the Kanjars are found over a large part of north India, their main concentration is in the western part of the upper and middle Ganga valley (25° 30' N : 77° 84'E.) which is administratively broadly equivalent to the present-day State of Uttar Pradesh (U.P.). Geographically it forms a part of the vast Indo-Gangetic plain of north India which is the most fertile and densely populated region in the country. The elevation of the plain above sea level, in the region under consideration, ranges from 275 m in the west to 60m in the east. The plain is drained by the Ganga and its numerous tributaries, some rising in the Himalayas to the north and others in the low hills of the peninsula to the south. The annual average rainfall ranges from around 800 mm in the west to around 1300 mm in the east. The natural vegetation cover is typical of the tropical dry deciduous woodlands. Steadily increasing population pressure and consequent human manipulation of the landscape over the last over six thousand years, and particularly since the beginning of the twentieth century, have almost completely obliterated the primary vegetation cover; today only a few characteristic plant species survive in heavily degraded and isolated pockets. However, even as late as fifty years ago large tracts of woodland existed in the plains. Wildlife was plentiful, especially blackbuck (*Antilope cervicapra*), chital (*Axis axis*), nilgai (*Boselaphus tragocamelus*), hyena (*Hyena hyena*), wolf (*Canis lupus*), fox (*Vulpes bengalensis*), jackal (*Canis aureus*) and porcupine (*Hystrix indica*). Herds of blackbuck numbering several hundred individuals could be commonly seen in the vicinity of villages. However, conversion of woodlands into farmland and the easy availability of guns after Independence have almost completely decimated the blackbuck and chital and considerably reduced the population of other species.

3. The data and its Sources

The most comprehensive account of the Kanjars is a paper by John C. Nesfield published in 1883. Brief accounts are also available in the successive census reports from 1871 onwards (Beverley 1872; Datta 1922; Egerton 1891); Gait 1892; Ibbetson 1883; Kaul 1912; Khan 1912; Kitts 1882; Maclagan 1892; Turner 1933; William 1869) and in the writings of A. Ayyangar (1951), B.S. Bhargava (1949, 1950), E.A.H. Blunt (1931), W. Crooke (1896), A.K. Das *et al.* (1966), R.E. Enthoven (1922), Stephen Fuchs (1969), R.P. Gondal (1937), J.H. Hutton (1951), T.S. Katiyar (1964), W. Kirkpatrick (1911a, 1911b, 1911c, 1913), E.D. Maclagan (1892), D.N. Majumdar (1944, 1947), U.B. Mathur (1969), H.H. Risley (1891), H.A. Rose (1911), R.V. Russell and R.B. Hira Lal (1916), P. Sharma (1959), and M.A. Sherring (1872). Apart from the account of Nesfield the four papers by Kirkpatrick have contributed original material on the language, folklore, social organisation and customs of the community. Crooke, Enthoven and Russell and Hira Lal summarised the available information on the community in the respective areas covered by their ethnographic surveys. The rest of the writings make only brief mention of the community on the basis of already known information. The only post-Independence studies of the community are two papers by M.K. Gautam (1983) and B.C. Jain (1980).

The present study is mainly based on the information available in these published sources. Though it describes the ethnographic situation as it existed between nearly 100 and 50 years ago, it is written in the present tense because much of the description still holds good. This is amply proven by the field data collected by me and V.N. Misra from the Kanjar settlements in Kuiyan village in Farrukhabad district and in Farrukhabad city. The major difference between the situation a century ago and now is that the forest in the plains has almost completely disappeared, and consequently the large game too has vanished. This has forced the Kanjars to give up their nomadic life style and settle down more or less permanently in colonies on the fringes of peasant settlements and towns. Enough small game is, however, still available in the cultivated fields and shrub covered riverine tracts to permit them to continue a certain degree of hunting activity.

4. Distribution

The Kanjars are among the largest and most widely distributed tribal communities of north India. They are found in all the plains districts of Uttar Pradesh as also in the hilly district of Mirzapur. Their concentration is, however, greatest in the western and central districts. Outside U.P. they are found in Punjab, Haryana, Jammu and Kashmir, Gujarat, Maharashtra, Madhya Pradesh, Bihar, West Bengal and Assam. The population of the community in U.P. in 1891 was 17,865. By 1971 it had increased to 44,176, that is by 147 percent. There has been no significant change in the overall distribution of the community from 1891 to 1971. However, population in some districts has declined while in others it has increased. This is obviously due to regional migration (Figs. 1 and 2).

5. Settlement Pattern

Today almost all the Kanjars are settled in exclusive colonies in the vicinity of villages and towns. Depending upon their economic condition they live in wattle huts, mud houses with thatched roofs, or brick houses. In the past, however, many of them lived a nomadic life, camping at one place for a few days, weeks or months, and then moving on to another. According to Nesfield (1883: 369) "All true Kanjars are addicted to a roving life; and if they halt for a time near some town or village, they put up their temporary sheds made with poles and matting, in a grove at some distance apart from the abodes of the settled inhabitants... Their natural home is the forest." The close association of the community with the forest is also exemplified in their marriage practice and disposal of the dead. The girl's father gives away to his son-in-law "...a patch of forest assumed to be his own, which becomes thenceforth the property of the bridegroom, so long as the encampment remains near this place, or whenever it may return to it. No one without the bridegroom's consent will be authorised to use this piece of forest either for hunting or for trapping, or for digging out the roots of *Khaskhas*, or for gathering wild honey, or collecting medical herbs" (Nesfield 1883: 382-383). Among the different methods of disposing of the dead prevalent in the community, one is to leave the corpse exposed in the forest.

The exact size of the nomadic groups is not always mentioned but it appears to have been small. According to Nesfield (1883: 370) the Kanjars "...are seldom or never seen in groups of more than 20 or 40 persons of all ages at any time, and the number is sometimes less. These little groups may unite sometimes for special and temporary objectives. But large groups are never permanently formed ... there are some groups or clans, which make a habit of keeping within easy reach, while others seldom or never leave the forest. But even among the former, it is not merely the proximity of settled communities, which prevents the formation of larger groups. For even in the wider forest tracts, where there is ample space and no impediment from higher races, the same law of petty non-associative hordes prevails; and it would be a rare thing to find an encampment of more than, or even as many as, 50 persons".

Many Kanjars have now settled down in permanent hamlets with fifteen or more families. One such settlements is located about a km. to the north of the Kuiyan village which lies about 10 km north of Farrukhabad city on the left side of the road connecting the city to the town of Allahganj. The families living in this hamlet eke out their living by hunting small game like fox, jackal, monitor lizard, and turtle, and collecting turtle eggs from the banks of the Ganga and Ramganga rivers. They sell the meat and skins to the people in the neighbouring villages. The skins are used for making shoes and other articles. Some children from this settlement attend school in the Kuiyan village.

Another large settlement, known as Khalula, is located on the sandy bed of the

Ganga, south of the army cantonment town of Fatehgarh. The inhabitants of this settlement are also exclusively engaged in hunting small game, mainly in the tamarix bushes in the rived bed. A number of persons from these settlements have now moved to Farrukhabad and Fatehgarh towns and have taken to petty trade, mostly carrying their wares like plastic bottles and other irtems of every day use on four-wheeled carts.

6. Physical Appearance, Dress and Ornaments

The Kanjars are markedly different in their physical appearance from the Proto-Australoid tribal communities of peninsular India as well as from many of the lower castes of the Ganga plains. They are tall, slim, well built and have high foreheads and sharp noses. In fact, but for their comparatively dark complexion they are little different from the upper caste Hindus of the region. Probably because of the high component of animal fat in their diet they have a healthier appearance than the other communities at the same economic level. Their hunting activity involves a lot of walking and running which helps them maintain a good physique. Many Kanjar males are very conscious of maintaining good health and are proud of their physical prowess. They are particularly fond of wrestling and some of them are champion wrestlers.

The dress and ornaments of the Kanjars are not very different from those of the other communities. Men usually wear *lungi* in place of *dhoti* worn by the people of Hindu caste groups, shirt, and sometimes turban. Women wear *saris* and *cholis* like the women of other communities. Both men and women are fond of ornaments which consist of a steel bangle and gold ear rings in the case of men, and gold ear rings and silver necklaces, bangles and anklets in the case of women.

7. Social Organisation

The name Kanjar, according to William Crooke, is probably derived form the Sanskrit *kanan char*, meaning 'dweller or wanderer in the forest'. The Kanjars are divided into a number of distinct groups. On the basis of information collected from many informants in different parts of U.P. Crooke has mentioned as many as 48 groups. Their names are as follows:

1. Badhik, 2. Baheliya, 3. Baid, 4. Baraiya, 5. Barua, 6. Beldar, 7. Beriya, 8. Bhains, 9. Bharu, 10. Bhantu, 11. Bohat, 12. Chamarmangta, 13. Chanal or Chandal, 14. Dhobibans, 15. Dom, 16. Ekthanliya, 17. Ghamra, 18. Ghasar, 19. Gohar, 20. Habura, 21. Jallad, 22. Jhinjhotiya, 23. Jogi, 24. Kabutarwala or Brijbasi, 25. Kanaujiya, 26. Kangiwala, 27. Kara, 28. Kedar, 29. Khatoniya, 30. Kuchband or Kunchband, 31. Lakarhar, 32. Lohiya, 33. Mariya, 34. Mattu, 35. Nat, 36. Pattari, 37. Pattharkat, 38. Qalandar, 39. Racchband, 40. Sankat, 41. Sansiya, 42. Singiwala, 43. Sirkiband, 44. Soda, 45. Son or Sonra, 46. Sonarsen, 47. Turkata, and 48. Untwar.

Some of these groups like the Badhik, Baheliya, Bhantu, Beriya, Dom, Habura, Jogi, Nat and Sansiya are distinct tribes or castes. It seems very likely that they have been included among the Kanjars on the basis of faulty information or because of their general similarity to the Kanjars in occupation, crime, social status, and vagrant way of life. Most of the Kanjars today stoutly deny any relationship with these communities.

The names of some others are obviously based on the occupation of the groups. For example, the Beldar wander about and work at digging tanks and building mud walls. The Bhains are buffalo-keepers. The Chamarmangta de-wax ears, perform cupping and extract carious teeth. The Gohar are those who catch *goh* or monitor lizards. The Jallad are executioners. The Kunchbandiya make the *kunch* or brush used by weavers for cleaning thread. They also make *sirki* or roofing mats, dig the *Khaskhas* grasss, twist rope, and hunt wolves and other animals. The Mariya are said to be worshipers of the goddess Mari. The Kangiwala make and sell *kangi* or combs. The Lakarhar, Lohiya, and Mattu work respectively in wood, iron and earth. The Pattharkat and Sankat are stone-cultters. The Qalandar train monkeys and bears to dance, and make articles of tin for sale. The Rachhband too, like the Kunchbandiya, are makers of weaver's brushes. The Turkata, who take their name from *tur* or weaver's brush, are quacks, and sell herbs and drugs which they collect in the jungle. The Singiwala and Baid are also quacks, collecting and selling herbs, and performing cupping.

Yet others, like the Kanaujiya, Jhinjhotiya, and Brijbasi are probably named after the regions from where they migrated to other places. Names like Ghamra, meaning lazy, and Chandal, meaning cruel and filthy, are probably given to them because of the peculiar habits of those groups.

The Kanjars are divided into many exogamous clans (*kuris*). The names of a few of the clans which we were able to collect during fieldwork are: Soda or Sanisoda, Dhirela or Bhuntiyarakhan, Rara, and Untwar. All clans appear to have equal status. Marriage alliances are usually preferred within clans and families which are already related by marriage. It is usual to find several brothers and cousins married in the same or related families of another clan. Polygamy, exchange marriage, divorce, re-marriage after divorce or death of the spouse are permitted for both men and women. In the case of a second marriage both levirate and sororate the preferred forms.

8. Subsistence

The Kanjars subsist largely on wild animal foods and are almost omnivorous in their diet. They kill and eat all kinds of creatures - terrestrial, avian and aquatic. They hunt jackal, fox, wolf, porcupine, jungle cat, hedgehog, hare, and monitor lizard. They trap or shoot squirrels and birds like pigeon, dove, partridge and quail. They also snare or kill turtles, and dig out snakes, mongooses, bandicoots, field rats, lizards, turtles and turtle eggs, "… and any other vermin that chance may throw their way" (Nesfield 1883: 369-370). They also scavenge carcasses of dead animals. "Whatever a Kanjars kills, from a wolf to a reptile, he eats; and most of what he finds dead, he eats also" (Nesfield 1883: 395). They also catch frogs both for their own consumption and for sale to school and college laboratories. Besides, they also gather and consume wild plant foods and extract juice from the palm-tree which when fermented forms an intoxicating drink. Besides animal flesh, the Kanjars consume milk, eggs, cereals, pulses, vegetables, etc.

9. Technology and Techniques of Hunting

The main tool and weapon of the Kanjars is the *khanta* or *Khanti* (Fig. 4). The name is supposed to be derived from the Sanskrit root *khan*, meaning to dig or make a hole. The tool consists of a long (about 1.2 m) wooden staff and an iron blade (about 30 cm long), either rectangular in shape **or** sharpened into a curved point something like the blade of a knife, and hafted at one end of the staff. The iron blade is procured by the Kanjars from the local iron-smiths and the staff is made by themselves. According to Nesfield, the implement serves as a dagger or short spear for killing wolves and jackals; as a tool for carving a secret entrance through the mud wall of a villager's house, where a burglary is contemplated; as a spade or hoe for digging out snakes, field rats, lizards, etc; for digging edible roots and the roots of *khaskhas* grass, and as a hatchet for chopping wood. It is used for dragging out monitor lizards and other creatures from the hollows in trees. The *khanti* or short spear is not merely used in close combat, but is also thrown with almost unerring effect when hunting wolves and jackals on the run.

Fig. 4. *Khanta/Khanti* used by the Kanjars for a variety of purposes

The *Khabar* (Fig. 5) is a large net used to snare wolves, jackals, foxes, porcupines, hares, etc. Woven from nylon string the *khabar* is about 12m long and 1.25m broad. It is stretched along the edge of a field of sugarcane or other tall crop or bushes of *munja* (*saccrum munja*) where the presence of animals has been identified beforehand. The *khabar* is supported at the base on a thick rope, and stretched vertically with sticks placed at intervals along its length. A group of Kanjars drive the animals from all sides of the field towards the net, thereby closing all escape routes so that the animals get trapped in the net.

The *suja*, a long spear, (Fig. 6) is used to kill turtles as well as other animals. The *khonch*, (Fig. 7) which consists of a cylindrical, open-mouthed cloth bag attached to a long bamboo pole, is used to catch frogs from wells and ponds.

According to Nesfield the Kanjars display extraordinary skill in the use of their simple weapons. The weapon with which they kill little birds is nothing but a pole with a thin sharp spike of iron embedded at the pointed end. The man lies motionless on a patch of ground, which he has first sprinkled with grain, and as the birds come hopping, he moves the pole in serpent-like motion, and then spikes the bird through its body. The Kanjars seldom or never use the bow and arrow, but they use a *gulel* or a pellet bow (Fig. 8) which requires much greater skill. The pellet is nothing but a little clay marble dried in the sun. With this they frequently shoot a sitting or flying bird. To trap a wolf in its lair, they place a net and a light at one end of the hole, and commence digging at the other end. The wolf attracted by the light runs into the net, and the Kanjar then batters its head with a club and kills it.

Fig. 5. *Khabar* used by the Kanjars for snaring wolves, jackals, etc.

Fig. 6. *Suja*, a long spear used by the Kanjars for killing turtles and other creatures

Fig. 7. *Khonch*, a cylindrical open-mouthed cloth bag used for catching frogs from wells & ponds

Fig. 8. *Gulel* or pellet bow used by the Kanjars for shooting birds

Their dogs are of great assistance to the Kanjars in their hunting activities and every family has two or more of them. The dogs are slim, agile and ferocious, and are carefully trained to hunt. They are extremely efficient in catching fleeing animals like the jackal, fox, jungle cat and hare.

10. Other Occupations

Besides hunting and gathering, the Kanjars practise a variety of other occupations, especially crafts, the products of which they sell to villagers and townspeople in exchange for grain, pigs, cloth, utensils, ornaments, etc. They are expert stone cutters and almost have a monopoly of making milling and grinding stones. They also undertake the pecking or sharpening of these objects which finds them regular and ready work among peasant homes throughout the year. A few decades ago, a Kanjar going round a village with his *khanti* on his shoulder, used to be a common sight. On the *khanti* was hung a basket which contained hammer and chisels for pecking milling and grinding stones and honey, grain, etc. As he moved through the village streets, he would loudly announce that he had honey for sale and was available for pecking stone objects and removing honey from beehives. However, with the introduction of diesel or electricity run commercial grinding mills the grinding of grain by traditional domestic grinding mills has virtually come to a stop except perhaps in very poor homes. Grinding stones are now used only for grinding turmeric and other spices.

The Kanjars make mats of *sirki* or *munj* (*Saccrum munja*) reeds, baskets of cane, hand-held fans of palm leaves for getting breeze during summer months, winnowing fans from *munj* stalks and rattles of plaited straw or reeds, the last sold to village children as toys. From the stalks of *munj* grass and from the fibre from the roots of *palas* (*Butea frondosa*) tree they make ropes. They also prepare a variety of rope items for use by the peasants in farming and other operations. These include nets for transporting wheat straw from the barn to home, and mouth covers for bullocks to prevent them from eating the grain during threshing. The Kanjars prepare skins of goats, jackals, foxes and monitor lizards to sell to leather workers. The goat skins are used to make drums, jackal and fox skins are used for making fur caps, and those of monitor lizards for making wallets, bags, shoes and other articles. The Kanjars also make plates and cups of *palas* leaves to sell to sweetmeat makers. Such plates and cups have a large market in towns and villages as they are used for serving food during wedding and other festive occasions. Besides, the Kanjars make rope nets for transporting straw from the barn to home and mouth covers to prevent bullocks from eating grain during threshing operations. The mats of *sirki* reeds, with which they cover their own temporary sheds, are largely used by cart drivers to protect their goods and themselves against rain. The toddy or juice of the palm tree which they extract and ferment, partly for their own use, finds a ready sale among low caste Hindus. The Kanjars are the chief stone cutters of north India and specialists in the manufacture of grinding stones which were used in every rural home but are now becoming obsolete. They gather the white wool-like fibre which grows in the pods of the *salmali* or silk-cotton tree and twist it into thread for weavers. They used to have an almost complete monopoly in the manufacture of brushes for cleaning cotton yarn and in the collection and sale of *khaskhas* grass for making screens that were widely used as room coolers during summer months before coolers and air conditioners became common. One of the major occupations of the Kanjars is collecting honey from wild beehives in the trees and from hives on the eves of rural thatched houses. They go around the villages looking for beehives and when they locate one in a villager's house, they ask permission to collect the honey, sharing it with the owner of the house. In addition, some of them keep livestock, mainly buffaloes, goats and poultry, and a very few engage in limited cultivation. Those who have moved to towns engage in small businesses like owning firewood stalls, selling plastic goods, and cheap footwear and other articles. In Bhogaon town in Mainpuri district a few Kanjars are big-time traders and own trucks.

11. Crime

A number of hunting-gathering communities of the plains, like the Aheriyas, Haburas and Sansiyas, have acquired considerable notoriety for their criminal activities like theft, burglary, highway robbery, dacoity and even murder. While the Kanjars are not as notorious, they are known to commit theft and highway robbery. Travellers are fearful of passing through lonely or sparsely inhabited tracts in the vicinity of Kanjar habitations. The British government had classified the Kanjars among the criminal tribes.

12. Disposal of the Dead

There are four modes of disposing of the dead among the Kanjars: (1) submersion in deep water by fastening a stone to the corpse; (2) cremation; (3) burial; and (4) leaving the corpse exposed in the jungle. Each clan disposes of its dead according to its hereditary custom. The first method, that is, submersion in water, is the least common, and the third, that is burial, is the one most frequently practised as well as most highly esteemed. A man who has acted as a spirit medium to *Mana* (the ancestral hero and deity) is invariably buried, no matter to whichever clan he may have belonged. In Aligarh district they usually bury their dead but sometimes expose corpses in the jungle. If buried, the corpse is laid with its feet to the north and head to the south. In *Etah* district they are said to be in the intermediate stage between burial and cremation, and both practices prevail.

13. Religion

The religion of the Kanjars, according to Nesfield, is without idols, shrines and formal priesthood. Their main deity is *Mana*, the ancestral hero, who is always benevolent. He is worshipped with more ceremony during the rainy season when the tribe is less migratory. On such occasions members of several bands unite temporarily to pay homage to their common ancestor. The worshippers collect near a tree under which they sacrifice a pig, a goat, a sheep, a fowl and a monitor lizard, and make an offering of roasted flesh and toddy. It is said that formerly they used to sacrifice a child after making him unconscious with toddy. They dance round the tree in honour of *Mana* and sing songs to commemorate his wisdom and deeds of valour. The Kanjars goddesses are *Mari*, *Parbha* and *Bhuiyan*. *Mari* is the goddess of death, *Parbha* or *Prabha* meaning light, is the goddesss of health, and *Bhuiyan* or *Bhawani* is the goddess of the earth.

All Kanjars live in fear of evil spirits, typified by the souls of the dead who are believed to enter the bodies of the living as a punishment for past misdeeds. All diseases as also death due to sickness or violence are ascribed to these evil spirits. When a patient is possessed by a spirit, the Kanjars employ an exorcist or spirit medium whom they call *Nyotiya* to drive away the spirit.

14. Acculturation

The Kanjars, like the other hunting-foraging communities, have been living in the midst of settled rural and urban people (primarily Hindus) for at least two millennia. Naturally they have had some contact with these technologically and economically more advanced communities. They have been influenced by the latter, and in turn have influenced them. This contact grew steadily closer as more and more forest was cleared for agriculture, settlements, roads and railway lines, industry, etc. In this process the original habitat of the Kanjars was steadily destroyed, and resources for hunting and foraging were reduced. From being totally nomadic the Kanjar bands had to settle down in the vicinity of villages and towns. Considerably deprived of their traditional sources of livelihood they had to make new adjustments in their subsistence strategies. This they did by adapting their traditional craft skills in rope making, reed working, hide processing, etc. to produce articles useful to the peasantry in their agricultural and other activities. By selling these articles to the villagers and townspeople they were able to earn some cash to buy from the markets items they needed like clothing and jewellery. In this way they were able to establish a symbiotic relationship with society at large. Some of them also took to crime as one of the alternative sources of livelihood. Along with this they have continued to practise hunting and foraging to the extent that reduced ecological resources permit them.

The social and religious organisation of the Kanjars has also undergone a change in this process of acculturation. They have adopted some of the Hindu deities for worship, and a few have also begun to use the services of the low grade Brahmin priests in their social and religious ceremonies. Even though they were totally independent people and completely outside the pale of the Hindu caste structure, their contact with Hindu society was bound to bring them, to some extent, into the caste fold. Because of their nomadic or semi-nomadic life, omnivorous diet, consumption of the flesh of animals considered unclean by the Hindus, general poverty and ignorance, and non-acceptance of Brahamanical rituals they were treated as untouchables. The British government branded them as a criminal tribe. After Independence they were declared as a denotified tribe, and more recently they have been grouped among the Scheduled Castes, a decision that gives official sanction to their low status in the society.

John Nesfield thought that communities like the Kanjars provided the source from which many of the artisan and other lower castes of Hindu society have been formed. It might be instructive to quote him at some length on this subject.

"In most of the arts or industries of the Kanjars it is easy to recognize functions or germs of functions, one or other of which has long been the stereotyped hereditary calling of certain inferior castes, such as Bahaliya, Bari, Behna, Chamar, Dharkar,

Kori, Kalwar, and others; and hence we may reasonably conclude, that the wandering and predatory tribes, which were once universal in Upper India, but of which now only a few fragments remain, were the *rudis indigestaque moles*, out of which the several castes, with their respective functions, were fashioned by slow degrees."

"What we see now of the Kanjar people is no doubt a mere fraction of what they formerly were; it is probable that, in the course of their history through the long centuries that have passed, their original tribal system, if they ever had one, has been shattered to pieces, and new groups have been formed at different times from the fragments that remained."

"This jungle nation is gradually dying out, or (to speak more correctly) is becoming more and more absorbed into the far mightier jungle of Indian caste, like the other great nations of this country, which were swallowed up centuries ago or are being swallowed up still. At the present time, for example, (and there are many parallel instances), several little encampments of Kanjars are dotted around Lucknow; and most of these have halted, where they still are, without a break for the last seven or eight years or more. These are gradually learning Hindu rites and forgetting their own. The Brahman, ever as keenly on the scent for fees as the Kanjar is for jackals, has found them out and is silently drawing them into the net, from which there is no escape. The day of their capture is not far distant."

"If admissibility into caste depends upon qualifications of function, then it is easy to see from the arts and industries in which Kanjars excel, that there are many low Hindu castes, into which they could be absorbed at once, if they would drop their tribal name, renounce their freedom, and consent to practise the same worship and the same marriage rites as those of the caste or castes into which they seek to enter. It is impossible to say how many of the caste men, who are now called Chamars, Koris, Pasis, Behanas, Baris, etc., were not originally Kanjars; or how many Kanjars may not have risen imperceptibly, at an earlier stage of their history, into the ranks of castes holding a much higher status than these in the social scale. There is one caste called Khangar, the members of which, if we are to trust the similarity of name, must have been Kanjars, not many years ago. They are a low and despised caste, still known as hunters and trappers in a small way, but chiefly employed as general drudges, field-labourers, night watchmen, and swineherds, a squalid, fever-stricken, spirit broken tribe, which has lost the healthy life, the versatile genius, and the happy freedom of their brethren of the forests" (Nesfield 1883: 397-398).

15. Recent Changes

After Independence the Kanjars were declared a Denotified Community (Ayyangar 1951) and officially freed from the stigma of being a criminal community. They were included among the Scheduled Castes and thus became entitled to preferential treatment in education, government employment, and economic betterment. Because of the total disappearance of forests in the plains all groups have now settled down in or near villages and towns. However, most of them continue to practise a certain degree of hunting-gathering, honey collecting, making and selling of rope articles, and other traditional activities. Because of their general poverty and social backwardness only a small section of the Kanjars has been able to take advantage of the educational and other facilities provided by the government. Some young people have received a college education and got jobs in various government departments. The more intelligent and enterprising members of the community have improved their economic condition. In recent years under various government schemes for the uplift of the weaker sections they have been provided with housing plots and agriculture land, and grants and loans for the purchase of livestock, agricultural equipment and other inputs, for building houses and starting businesses. Some of those living in cities have taken to trading in factory-made goods, specially plastic items. They sell their wares in towns on hand carts propelled on four cycle wheels and in the villages on bicycles. A few have taken to trade on a larger scale, for example the sale of fuel wood and timber or taken jobs in power-operated flour grinding mills. A few Kanjars in Bhogaon, a town in Mainpuri district are engaged in the transport business, own trucks, live in large *pucca* (made of brick and cement) houses and are quite wealthy.

By and large the community is slowly becoming conscious of its rights and privileges under various government schemes and is claiming a higher social status. In Farrukhabad town a group of educated Kanjar youth claiming to belong to the Bhoksa tribe of the Uttaranchal hills managed to get certificates to that effect from some elected representatives. The more aggressive among the Kanjars claim to be the descendants of the ancient rulers of the region and assert that some of the well-known archaeological sites are ruins of the former capitals of their kings. Slowly but steadily the lot of the community is improving. One major hurdle in their economic and social improvement is the high birth rate in the community and its general reluctance to adopt family planning methods. However, it is certain that with the passage of time they will completely give up their hunting-gathering activities and take to socially more acceptable vocations.

16. Relevance for Social History

Equally significant is the Kanjar evidence for understanding the process whereby hunter-foragers have been assimilated into settled society. As their habitat shrank due to the clearance of the forests by settled people, the hunter-foragers were forced to come into contact with the latter. While continuing their traditional subsistence strategies with reduced re*sources they had to increasingly take to other occupations to ensure their survival in an altered and impoverished environment. They established a certain degree of symbiotic relationship with various caste groups by supplying them with their craft products, honey and hunted game in exchange for grain, animals, and cash. They were also drawn into the social network of the caste system though only in a peripheral manner. The members of many of the artisan and service castes of Hindu society have probably been recruited from indigenous communities like the Kanjars. The process of the ongoing integration of the Kanjars into the larger society therefore provides us with an insight into the evolution of the complex Hindu social system.

17. Conclusion

The Kanjars are one of the many hunting-foraging communities still surviving in the alluvial plains of north India. These communities are almost certainly descended from the pioneering Mesolithic colonisers of these plains. Although the steady destruction of their jungle habitat by settled rural and urban populations over several millennia has greatly transformed their lifestyle, they still retain many elements of a hunting-foraging way of life in their subsistence strategies, settlement pattern, language, folklore, social organisation and religion. Valuable information about them is available in the writings of British and Indian officials and ethnographers of the later part of the nineteenth and early part of the twentieth century. This information can provide archaeologists with significant insight into the reconstruction of the lifeways of Mesolithic societies. It is equally or even more useful for social historians to understand the process of the integration of indigenous peoples into the caste system. So far this valuable reservoir of information has been little exploited by archaeologists and historians, and today hardly any original field research is being done on them. The Kanjars and other related groups therefore deserve better attention from archaeologists and historians than they have received so far.

RAJASTHAN

1. Introduction

Rajasthan, the largest state of the Indian Union, following the bifurcation of Uttar Pradesh and Madhya Pradesh to form Uttarakhand and Jharkhand, respectively, is divided by the Aravalli Hills, which run in a northeast-southwest direction from Delhi to north of Ahmedabad, into two unequal and markedly distinct geographical regions. The eastern part, the southeastern part of which is known as Mewar, is largely hilly and rocky, receives adequate, though occasionally irregular, rainfall, is drained by the Chambal and its large tributary network, is agriculturally more productive and fairly densely populated. The western part, much of which consists of Marwar (roughly equivalent to former Princely State of Jodhpur) and Thar desert (broadly equivalent to former princely states of Jaisalmer and Bikaner), is characterized by the absence of perennial streams, scanty and erratic rainfall, extreme scarcity of potable water, hot windy and dusty summers, sand-dune covered and rocky landscape, and sparse human population. Because of these environmental conditions agriculture plays only a limited role in the rural economy. It is only in the region known as Godwar near the Aravallis (broadly Pali and part of Sirohi districts), which receives higher rainfall, is free from sand dunes, and where fresh water is available though at considerable depth, that winter or *rabi* cultivation is possible. Over the rest of the region only one annual crop, *kharif,* is grown during the rainy season. In the hyper-arid extreme western and northern parts of the desert hardly any cultivation can be practised. In spite of low precipitation dune surfaces support rich grass and shrub vegetation which provides ample pasture for wild herbivores and livestock. The mainstay of the rural economy is therefore pastoralism which consists of the breeding of cattle, sheep, goat, and camels. Because of frequent droughts famines are common and both animal and human populations are obliged to migrate periodically to more congenial areas outside the desert.

Though, at present, the environmental conditions in the desert are very inhospitable, they were much better in the past, specially during the Middle and early Upper Pleistocene, and early and middle Holocene (Singh *et al.* 1974; Singhvi 2003; Deotare *et al.* 2003). Archaeological research has shown that the antiquity of human settlement in the desert goes back to the later half of the Middle Pleistocene. Many Lower, Middle and Upper Palaeolithic sites have been located, particularly around Didwana in Nagaur district (Misra and Rajaguru 1989). A number of Late Acheulian and Middle Palaeolithic sites have been located in the Luni Valley (Misra 1962), and some Middle Palaeolithic sites have been found in Jaisalmer district in the hyper-arid part of the desert (Allchin *et al.* 1978; Misra and Rajaguru 1989). However, Upper Palaeolithic sites are comparatively scarce as this period coincided with the very dry climate of the later part of the Upper Pleistocene.

There was significant proliferation of human populations during the early and middle Holocene due to increased rainfall and consequent increase in plant and animal food resources (Singh *et al.* 1974). Many Mesolithic sites are known including from the core of the desert. One of them, Tilwara in Barmer district, was excavated by V.N. Misra (1971) and has yielded a rich, highly developed geometric microlithic industry on chert and quartz, and a small quantity of bones of wild animals. In the upper levels of the site wheel made pottery and fragments of iron were found along with microliths, suggesting the survival of microlithic technology well into the Iron Age.

All through the Palaeolithic and Mesolithic periods the subsistence economy of human groups was based on hunting and gathering. Most of the western part of the State was too dry for farming-based settled life to appear during the Neolithic and Chalcolithic periods as it did in many parts of the country. The only exception was the Ghaggar river valley in the extreme north-west where Early Harappan culture appeared around five thousand years ago and was followed by the Mature Harappan culture (Lal 1997; Misra 2007). This was possible because the Rigvedic Saraswati, now represented by the dry bed of the Ghaggar), was perennially flowing in this region. Ochre-Coloured Pottery (OCP), which is equated with the Late Harappan culture, has been found from numerous sites in Jaipur, Sikar, Jhunjhunu and Bharatpur districts, suggesting that following the desiccation of the Saraswati, the Late Harappans migrated eastward. We have got some idea of the ceramics, copper technology and architecture of the OCP culture from excavations at Jodhpura in Jaipur district and Ganeshwar in Sikar district. In the rest of the western part of the State agriculture-based life was introduced only about two thousand years ago or even later, and people continued to live by hunting-gathering.

The eastern part of the State also has an equally long history of human occupation going back to the Lower Palaeolithic period. Plentiful remains of Lower Palaeolithic artefacts have been found from the alluvial deposits of the Chambal an Banas rivers and their tributaries like the Berach, Gambhiri, Wagan, Parvati and Kali Sind. Middle Palaeolithic, however, is known only from small assemblages from the Wagan and Kadmali valleys in southern Mewar, and there is no clear evidence of the Upper Palaeolithic. The Mesolithic stage of this region is much better known because a large number of microlithic sites have been found, particularly in Mewar, and excavations at the site of Bagor in Bhilwara district have provided very rich evidence of the hunting-gathering way of life, and transition from stone technology to copper and subsequently iron technology, and from hunting-gathering-herding to increasingly pastoral way of life (Misra 1973, 2007). In the eastern region, particularly in Mewar, agriculture-based settled life started around 3500 B.C. Here over 100 sites of the Chalcolithic Ahar culture have been found, and five of them, namely Ahar, Gilund (*IAR* 1959-60), Balathal (Misra 1997), Ojiyana (Meena and Tripathi 2001) and Lachhura (*IAR* 1998-99: 138-141) have been excavated. They have provided us a very detailed picture of the life of the pioneering farmers. This picture includes residential and defensive architecture made of stone, mud-brick and mud, copper technology, an economy based on the cultivation of a variety of summer and winter crops, domestication of animals, and a certain amount of hunting, advanced ceramic technology, represented by well-baked and richly decorated ceramics, terracotta animal figurines, beads of semi-precious stones, steatite and terracotta, and a few human burials At all these sites Chalcolithic culture was succeeded, after a hiatus, by iron age early historic culture.

Iron technology appeared in the northeastern part of the State towards the end of the second millennium B.C. The earliest iron comes from the site of Noh near Bharatpur and is associated with Black-and-Red ware ceramic as at Jodhpura in Jaipur district and at Atranjikhera in Etah district in U.P. The Black-and-Red Ware culture was succeeded by the well-known Painted Grey Ware (PGW) culture which is represented at many sites in the Upper Ganga-Yamuna doab and the Indo-Gangetic Divide. Some of these sites are associated with the story of the *Mahabharata* epic.

In both regions hunting-gathering way of life has survived right into the present. The principal hunting-gathering communities are Van Vagris, Kal Beliyas and Bhils. The Kal Beliyas and Bhils are found on both sides of the Aravallis but the Van Vagris are found only in the western part. While the Bhils and Kal Beliyas were studied by me during the early 1960s when I was doing field work around Udaipur, and again during the 1990s while I was participating in the excavations at the Chalcolithic site of Balathal near Udaipur, the Van Vagris were studied by V.N. Misra and the account of this community is based on his publications (Misra 1990).

We give below brief accounts of the culture of each of these communities, with the main emphasis on their hunting practices.

2. Van Vagris

The Van Vagris (also pronounced as Van Vavris or Van Vaoris) are a semi-nomadic hunting community found in parts of the semi-arid region of western Rajasthan. Probably because of their nomadic lifestyle, minimal contact with settled rural and urban communities, and shy and law-abiding nature, they have failed to attract the attention not only of researchers but also of the administration and development officials. One does not find any mention, let alone any description, of the community either in the official literature like census reports and gazetteers or in the few ethnographic publications on Rajasthan. The present account of the community is largely of a preliminary nature and needs to be enlarged by further field work.

2.1 Are the Van Vagris an Independent Ethnic Group?

There are two other communities in Rajasthan, namely Bagris and Baoris, whose names bear close phonetic resemblance with that of the Van Vagris. This similarity may suggest the possibility that the Van Vagris are identical with one or both of them. However, a comparison of the distribution and lifestyle of the three communities clearly shows that there is little in common between the Van Vagris on the one hand, and the Bagris and Baoris on the other, and that the former are an independent ethnic group.

The Gazetteer of Western Rajputana (Erskine 1909: 162-63) lists Baoris and Bagris among the eight criminal tribes of Jodhpur State. The Baoris were found in Merta, Nagaur, Jaitaran and Bilara parganas (parts of present-day Nagaur and Jodhpur districts), while the Bagris were found in Jalor and Jaswantpura *parganas* (Jalor and Jodhpur districts). Both in respect of the number of crimes committed and the percentage of population engaged in crime the Baoris were far ahead of the Bagris. Both communities were sedentary, practised agriculture, and possessed land and livestock. The Baoris were also found in Bikaner State and enjoyed similar reputation regarding their criminal activities. In Mewar (eastern Rajasthan) there were only two criminal tribes, namely Baoris and Moghias (other writers consider them to be identical), the Bagris being completely absent (Erskine 1908: 80). Here too they lived in villages alongside other communities, practised agriculture, and possessed livestock.

More recent references to Baoris and Bagris are available in the *Ethnographic atlas of Rajasthan*, a publication of the Census Department of the Government of India, based on 1961 census (Mathur 1969). In this work both these communities are included among Scheduled Castes, and classified as "castes traditionally associated with criminal activities". The Bagris are described as formerly being a wandering criminal tribe living by hunting and gathering but now settled and living by agriculture, animal husbandry and working as labourers. They are found in fourteen districts all of which, except Sirohi and Jalor, are in eastern Rajasthan (Mathur 1969: 74-75). In the same work the Baoris (also called Bawarias and Moghias) and described as a "community notorious for its criminal activities" but now largely settled as agriculturists. Most of them are concentrated in ten districts on both sides of the Aravallis (Mathur 1969: 72-73). Yet another census publication (Katiyar 1964: 3-7) describes the Bagris as followers of Hindu religion and lists agriculture, service and *chowkidari* (watchmanship) as their chief occupations. None of the works cited above nor another recent ethnographic study by Mathur (1986) makes any mention of the Van Vagris.

Against this background, the reasons cited below incline us to believe that the Van Vagris are an altogether independent and as yet unrecorded people with no connection with either the Bagris or the Baoris.

1. According to all the Hindu informants as also from Misra's interaction with a number of Van Vagris, the members of this community have an impeccable reputation for honest living and are law-abiding and peaceful by nature. The Bagris and Baoris, on the other hand, have both been classified as criminal tribes or castes in the literature, and are believed by the many people questioned, to have a tendency towards criminal activities.

2. The Van Vagris are a semi-nomadic community. Some of them settle down temporarily when they are employed as crop watchers by the local Hindu farmers. They do not build permanent structures and never stay within or even close to a village or town. The Bagris and Baoris, on the other hand, are sedentary groups living with other castes in permanent villages.

3. The Van Vagris live mainly by hunting and foraging and with rare exceptions they neither possess land nor engage in cultivation. They do not even like to work as labourers. The Bagris and Baoris, on the contrary, both practise agriculture and maintain livestock.

4. The Van Vagris, like many other hunting-foraging groups, bury their dead while the Bagris and Baoris, like other Hindu castes, cremate them.

5. And finally, on the basis of the genealogical data collected by Misra from Van Vagri informants, this community is found in Nagaur, Sikar, Churu and Ajmer districts. The Bagris, at least according to census records, are completely absent in the first three of these districts (Mathur 1969: 74-75). If the Bagris were the same people as the Van Vagris, it is inconceivable that they would have completely escaped enumeration by census operators in all these three districts when they were enumerated in more than nine other districts of the State. On the contrary, it seems more than likely that the Van

Vagris because of their nomadic nature and confinement to sandy country away from permanent settlements were found to be an inconvenient subject by census enumerators. The Baoris are, of course, present in the districts in which the Van Vagris are found, but they cannot be confused with the latter for reasons already mentioned.

The late Shri Komal Kothari, Director of Rupayan Sansthan, Jodhpur, and an acknowledged expert on the peoples of western Rajasthan, has confirmed the above assessment. In a very informative communication to V.N. Misra he said that the Bagris and Baoris have nothing to do with the Van Vagris and that the Bagris are not to be found in Nagaur-Didwana area (the area in which Misra collected the data on the Van Vagris). The Bagris, according to Shri. Kothari's information, are nomadic, providing certain services to the settled population. They would particularly appear at the time of feasts and collect the left-overs. The Baoris, on the other hand, are a settled people. During the rule of the Rajput princes they were a part of the administrative system, acting as *chowkidars* (watchmen) of the villages. They were not paid any salary for their services but were allowed by the local *jagirdar* (feudal lord subordinate to the ruler) to commit theft outside their region. However, when the British Government persuaded the Rajput princes to introduce regular administration with paid functionaries, the Baoris lost their traditional role and took to crime as their main source of livelihood.

About the Van Vagris Shri Kothari says that in Nagaur he did find people referring to Van Vagris, but work for them was to keep away the *rojh* (*nilgai* or blue bull, *Boselaphus tragocamelus*). He further says that several villages in Jodhpur district have one or two families of a community whom local people call Jangaliya (wild or forest-dweller) or, sometimes, Shikariya (hunter), but who call themselves Ahedi. The Jangaliya reside outside the village and practically live on hunting. They also protect the crops from *rojh* for which they are paid by the farmers in kind. This description fits in perfectly with Misra's information on the Van Vagris in Nagaur district. The Aheri (or Ahedi), according to census records (Mathur 1969: 94-95), are also known as lower class Thoris. They "once used to live solely as hunters and fowlers and beg with the Bhangis on the occasion of an eclipse. They have now taken to agriculture". Though found in more than ten districts (including Nagaur) of Rajasthan, the Aheris were mainly concentrated in the districts of Kota, Jhalawar, Udaipur and Chitorgarh.

About the Aheris of Punjab, Ibbetson (1916: 277) says: "The Aheris or Heris or Thoris are by heredity hunters and fowlers.... They are vagrant in their habits, but not infrequently settle down in villages where they find employment. They catch and eat all sorts of wild animals, pure and impure, and work with reeds and grass. In addition to these occupations they work in the fields, and especially move about in gangs at harvest time in search of employment as reapers; and they cut wood and grass and work as general labourers, and on roads and other earthworks. In Sirsa they occasionally cultivate, while in Karnal they often make saltpetre, and in Rajputana they are employed as outdoor servants, and even as musicians. Their home is Rajputana, and especially Jodhpur and the prairies of Bikaner.... They are considered outcasts, and made to live beyond the village ditch". In this description of Aheris there is much that holds true for Van Vagris as well; the only major difference is that while the Van Vagris bury their dead, the Aheris cremate them. This, however, is not difficult to understand as many former primitive tribes of the north Indian plains are slowly replacing burial by cremation, obviously as a consequence of contact with their dominant Hindu neighbours. This was, for example, the case, towards the end of the nineteenth century, among the Aheriyas of the North-West Provinces (present-day Uttar Pradesh) who, in the opinion of W. Crooke (1896 I: 40,44), are akin to the Aheris of Punjab and Rajasthan. It is also significant that in Ibbetson's description no mention is made of crime in relation to the Aheris.

Another community from the Punjab described by Ibbetson (1916: 275-76) and pertinent to the present context is that of the Bawarias. "The Bawarias are a hunting tribe who take their name from the *bawar* or noose with which they snare wild animals.... In addition to hunting they make articles of grass and straw and reeds and sell them to the villagers. The Bawarias are a vagrant tribe whose proper home appears to be Mewar, Ajmer, and Jodhpur; in the Panjab they are chiefly found along the middle Satluj valley in Sirsa, Firozpur, Faridkot, Lahore, and Patiala, though they occur in smaller numbers in Hissar, Rohtak, and Gurgaon, all on the Rajputana border.... They are by no means always, or indeed generally criminal, in this Province at least; and in Lahore and Sirsa seem to be sufficiently inoffensive. But in many parts of the Panjab, and generally I believe in Rajputana, they are much addicted to crime". Like the Aheris, the Bawarias also burn their dead.

V.N. Misra thinks it plausible that Van Vagris, Jangaliyas, Aheris, Bawarias (and perhaps others) are different local names of one and the same community which in the remote past lived only by hunting and gathering and was widespread in the plains of north India. Very likely they are descendants of Mesolithic hunting-gathering populations whose cultural remains have been found extensively in Rajasthan and the adjoining areas (Misra 2007). With the passage of time populations adapted to different ecozones would have developed their own cultural traditions and acquired separate names, perhaps from their more developed neighbours. Even the Bagris and Baoris of Rajasthan who are now reported to be completely settled may originally have been part of this ancestral population. However, as the agricultural way of life spread through these plains, and forests were cleared, the wild animal and plant food resources were reduced. As a consequence some of these ancestral hunter-gatherers must have taken to agriculture. Others would appear to have persisted with their traditional mode of subsistence by redefining their adaptive strategy to suit the changed natural and social environment. They entered into a symbiotic relationship with the peasantry by using their traditional craft skills to provide goods needed by the farmers, and by offering their services as labourers, watchmen, entertainers, etc. Yet others who were unable or unwilling to peacefully adjust to the new social order took to crime as a major source of livelihood.

2.2 Sources of Data

Most of the information pertaining to the distribution, social organisation and religion of the community was provided to Misra by Bhagu, a 70 year old man temporarily living outside Barangna village, 12 km south of Didwana, where one of his sons, Rauto, had taken on a crop watching job. Bhagu had a phenomenal memory and was an extremely patient and cooperative informant. His genial wife, Dhannodi and daughter-in-law, Sokuri were almost equally helpful and informative. The genealogical data provided by them formed the basis for learning about the distribution, clan organisation, family, and marriage practices of the community. This information was supplemented by Bhagwanyo, a young Van Vagri, temporarily settled during the same period outside Sundrasan village, 27 km east of Didwana. Data on hunting was collected through participation in hunting expeditions with Mohanyo, a young man engaged in crop watching at Baklia village, 25 km north of Didwana, and his brother-in-law, Samalyo, son of Bhagu referred to above, and by talking to them and a number of other Van Vagri and non-Van Vagri informants.

2.3 Habitat, Demography and Settlement Pattern

In the absence of any census data on the Van Vagris we do not know the exact area of their distribution. The information provided by the informants in the villages around Didwana gives only a partial picture of their distribution and population. The community is densely concentrated in the Nagaur, Didwana and Parvatsar tahsils of Nagaur district and in the Sikar tahsil of Sikar district. Their presence is also reported in Ajmer, Churu, Jodhpur and Jhunjhunu districts, and less certainly, in Bikaner district as well. Beyond Rajasthan they are known to be present in the contiguous districts of Rohtak and Mahendragarh in Haryana. Thus the present known distribution shows the community to be confined to the semi-arid and arid regions of the central and northern parts of west Rajasthan and the bordering region of Haryana (Fig. 9).

The Van Vagri habitat is an undulating plain formed of stabilized sand sheets and sand dunes. There are no streams or other natural water bodies in the area. In spite of low and unreliable rainfall (annual average 250-500 mm) the land supports a good vegetation cover. The tree par excellence of the region is *khejri (Prosopis cineraria)* which is well distributed both on cultivated and uncultivated land. Less common trees are *khair (Acacia catechu) baund/babul (Acacia arabica nilotica)* and *bordi (Zizyphus jujuba)*, the last a bush which also grows to small tree size. Common shrubs are *kheenp (Leptadenia pyrotechnica)*, *munj (Saccrum munja)*, *jhal (Salvadora oleoides)*, *sania* and *phog (Calligonum ploygonoides)*. Wildlife is quite plentiful. Blackbuck (*Antilope cervicapra*) and chinkara (*Gazella gazella*) were once abundant but are now found in large herds only around Bishnoi villages where they are protected by a strong religious sentiment. Nilgai are seen everywhere. Small game includes the fox (*Vulpes bengalensis*), jackal (*Canis aureus*), porcupine (*Hystrix indica*), hare (*Lepus nigricollis*), mongoose (*Herpestes edwardsi*), hedgehog (*Hemichinus auritus*), monitor lizard (*Varanus bengalensis* and *griseus*), and a large variety of birds among which the partridge (*Francolinus pondicerianus*) and sandgrouse (*Pterocles exustus erlanger*) are the most common.

Because of low rainfall and an almost complete absence of any means of irrigation there is only one effective agricultural season, and the arable land lies fallow for eight months of the year. Besides this, there still remain large tracts of uncultivated land which are used as pasture for livestock. The environment is thus ideally suited to support a rich variety of wildlife and therefore to sustain a hunting-gathering economy.

In the Didwana region the Van Vagris are to be found in the vicinity of around a hundred villages in an area of about 350 sq km. In this area it was possible to collect the names of around 450 men, women and children. This figure emerges from the genealogies of only two lineages of two clans and, not being an actual census, the figure does not represent the total Van Vagri population even of this limited area. The total population of the community in its entire habitat is likely to be several thousand individuals.

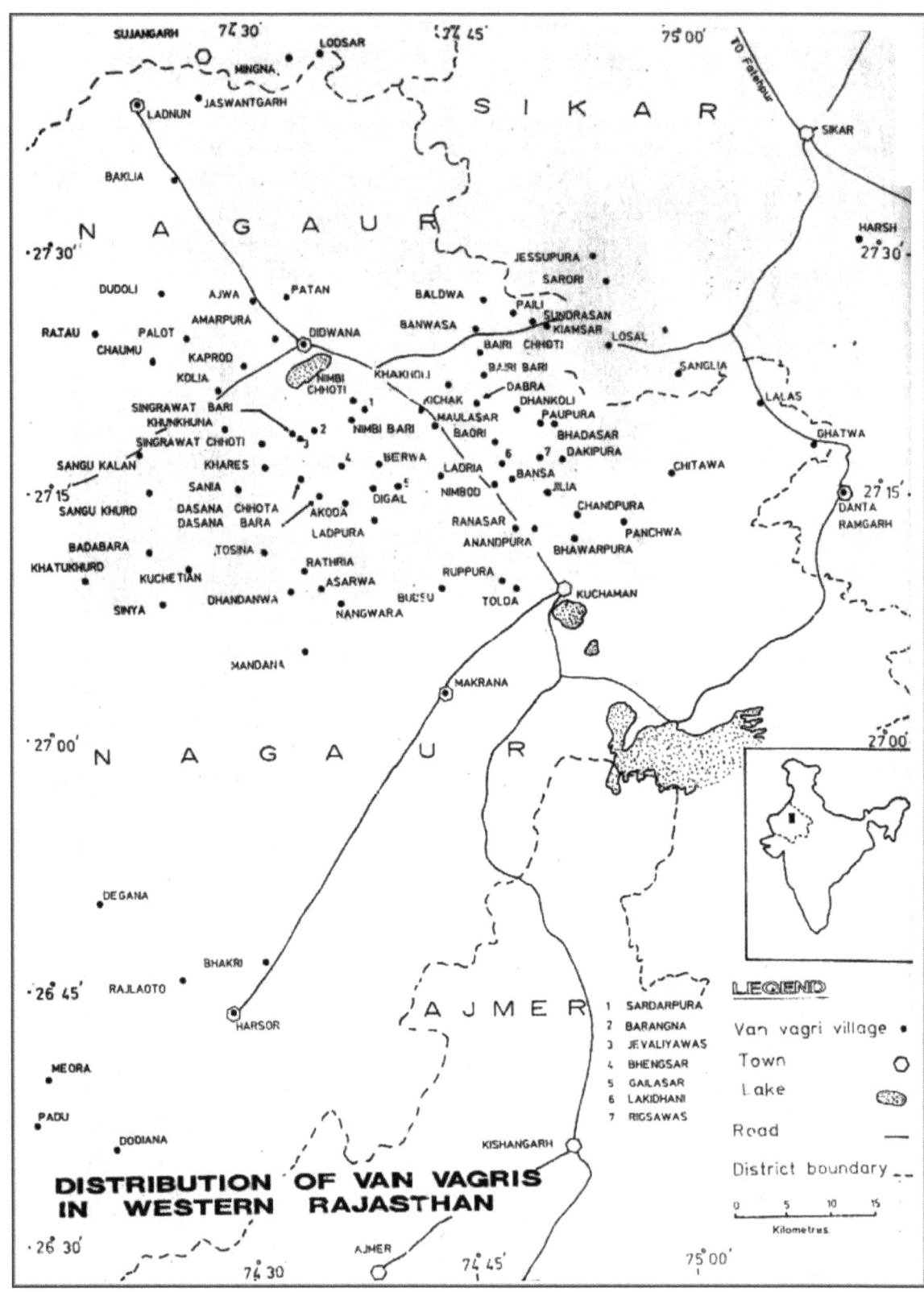

Fig. 9. Distribution of Van Vagris in the Didwana Area, Nagaur district

The Van Vagris live a nomadic life and spend most of their time in the *kankar* or *roi* (uncultivated or fallow land away from permanent settlements). They move in small bands of three to five families which are related by consanguineal or affinal ties. During their wanderings they camp for a few days at one place and are then on the move again. The camp is located on a sand dune or on the bank of a *naadi* (water tank) away from permanent settlements. During the dry season they live in the open, but during the rainy season they sometimes make small huts of tree branches, thorny twigs and grass, mainly to keep their meagre belongings and for small children to sleep in (Fig. 10). Every family has a semi-permanent base to which it periodically returns from its wanderings. However, when asked to name the village he belongs to, a Van Vagri is greatly puzzled, and he will at best name a few villages in the vicinity of which he spends the greater part of his annual life cycle. Few Van Vagris have housing plots of their own and they usually camp on public land.

Fig. 10. Van Vagri huts near Baklia village, north of Didwana

Their annual movement cycle takes place within an area of about 50 km radius. During winter when many Van Vagri males are engaged in crop watching for local farmers, they settle down with their families for three to four months at one place. They camp outside the village and raise small, temporary huts or just heaps of grass which serve as windbreaks. A few persons who have settled down live away from the village in wattle and daub huts. Whether moving or temporarily settled, the Van Vagris live most of their life under the sky. All their normal functions like cooking, eating, sleeping and even their sexual activities are performed in the open.

2.4 Physical Appearance, Dress and Ornaments

The Van Vagris are a medium to tall, slenderly built and handsome people of medium dark complexion. They have sharp noses, high foreheads and dark wavy hair). Except for their complexion they hardly look different from the other communities of the region. However, they certainly look quite distinct from the Proto-Australoid tribal peoples of peninsular India. The men wear *dhoti* up to knees, shirt, small turban and shoes (Fig. 11).

Fig. 11. A Van Vagri family with several children and their dog

Their clothes are mostly plain white. As ornaments some men wear bead and metal necklaces. Women, on the other hand, like those of other communities, are more colourfully dressed. They wear a *ghaghra* (skirt), *choli* (blouse), and *odhni* (a rectangular piece of printed cloth covering the head and the upper part of the body). Their ornaments include metal anklets, glass and plastic bangles, glass bead and metal necklaces, *bor* (an oval metal object worn just above the forehead in the parting of the hair), ear rings and a nose pin. Young girls wear similar clothes without the *odhni* (Fig. 12).

Fig. 12. Bhagu and his family at Varangana village near Didwana

2.5 Temperament and Character

The Van Vagri is a remarkably truthful, honest and sincere person. Because of his poverty, insecurity, and ignorance he is usually suspicious of strangers, but once a stranger is able to win a Van Vagri's confidence, he will find him a very warm, friendly, and generous person. On several occasions Misra had very touching experiences of their warmth and generosity. None of the informants or their family members ever asked for any payment in cash or kind for providing information or allowing themselves and their belongings to be photographed. This behaviour of theirs is in sharp contrast to that of other tribal and lower caste communities in the region.

2.6 Social Organisation

Van Vagri society is divided into a number of exogamous clans. In the Didwana area Misra was able to ascertain the names of 13 clans, but enquiries in other areas will probably reveal the existence of some more. These clans are: 1. Solanki, 2. Chauhan, 3. Rathor / Rathori, 4. Jamiyan/Diya, 5. Puanr, 6. Badgujar, 7. Karbiya, 8. Hada, 9. Khakariya, 10. Dhudhadia, 11. Bagad, 12. Igotia, and 13. Belda. Several of these names are identical with Rajput clan names and have no doubt been borrowed from them, as is done by most other tribes and lower castes in Rajasthan. All clans are generally equal in status though the Solankis consider themselves superior to others. Bhagu of the Solanki clan told Misra that clans whose members partake of *mosar* (death feast) are considered inferior and non-*mosar* eating clans will not have marriage alliances with the former.

The main function of the clan as a social unit appears to be in regulating marriages. It is too large and geographically diffused a group to play a significant role in other aspects of life. Instead, it is the lineage (a unit of the clan the members of which can actually trace their relationship to each other and to a common ancestor) that plays an important role in regulating life. On all important social and religious occasions it is the members of the lineage who come together to share joy and sorrow. However, the most important social unit is the family which is invariably of the nuclear type. After marriage a son sets up his own household and a daughter goes to live with her husband. There is a strong sense of economic independence in the Van Vagri family. Every family, whether of a newly married couple or of old parents, is expected to provide for itself and not make demands on another family. Even a married girl visiting her parents for a few days is expected to bring her own provisions and cook her food separately. A number of nuclear families constitute a band which plays a part in an individual's life next only to that of the nuclear family. A typical band consists of three to five families which are related by blood or marriage ties. The composition of the band is flexible, and individual families keep leaving one band and joining another. The inclusion of an individual in a band depends on his acceptability to heads of other families in the band. Male members of the band cooperate in hunting and the sharing of meat while females go together to the villages to beg for food and sell birds and animals brought by their men from the hunt. Band members share a common social life and help each other in times of need. Lasting friendships and emotional ties are forged among the members of a band.

2.7 Marriage

An individual can marry into any clan other than his own. In actual practice, however, there is a definite preference for certain clans and particular lineages within those clans while looking for spouses for sons and daughters. This is because families already related by marriage know the other families in their lineages. The usual age of marriage is around 20 years for males and around 15-16 years for females. The marriage alliance is usually negotiated by the parents of the prospective spouses, but if a boy and a girl fall in love with each other they are allowed to marry. This usually happens when the families of the boy and girl are members of the same band or, in case they belong to different bands, their *deras* (camps) are close by and they have frequent opportunity to meet and know each other. If there is resistance to the alliance from the parents of one or both parties, the boy and girl elope and seek refuge in the band of some relative, and eventually the parents reconcile and accept their marriage. Bride price is invariably paid by the boy's father to the girl's family. Bride price is waived when two men of different clans marry each other's sisters (exchange marriage).

Both bigamy and polygamy are accepted and there are several recorded cases of such marriages. Divorce is allowed for both men and women. If a woman is unhappy with her husband and has a liking for another man, she can desert the former and start living with the latter. The resulting friction is usually sorted out by the other man paying an amount equivalent to bride price to the husband. Widows are not only allowed, but indeed expected to remarry. A widow is required to marry her husband's younger brother or cousin (levirate) and a widower his wife's younger sister or cousin (sororate). Even when a man seeks another wife during the lifetime of his first wife, he prefers to marry his wife's younger sister. Because of the freedom enjoyed by men, and women in conjugal matters adultery is rare, but when it does take place both parties are punished by the *panchayat* (clan council).

2.8 Subsistence and Economy

The principal component of the Van Vagri diet is meat which he obtains by hunting and trapping wild animals and birds. He does not have many inhibitions about the creatures he kills and consumes. Indeed in the popular image the Van Vagri is omnivorous. Among the animals he hunts and eats are: sambar (*Cervus unicolor*), nilgai (*Boselaphus tragocamelus*), hiran (*Antilope cervicapra*), chinkara (*Gazella gazella*), wild boar (*Sus scrofa cristatus*), lunkhri (*Vulpes bengalensis*), gadhdo (*Canis aureus*), khargosh (*Lepus nigricollis*), sevli (*Hystrix indica*), javalya (*Hemichinus auritus*), mongoose (*Herpestes edwardsi*), guhera (*Varanus bengalensis*), gophalda (*Varanus griseus*), and wild cat (*Felis chaus*).

The birds hunted and eaten by the Van Vagris include teetal (*Francolinus pondicerianus*), batbad (*Pterocles exustus erlangeri*), kamedi (*Streptopelia decaocto decaocta*), kabutar (*Columba livia intermedia*), hariyal (*Treron phoenicoptera*), shikra (*Accipiter badius dussumieri*), mor (*Pavo cristatus*), gidh (*Gyps fulvus*), kurj (*Grus grus*), jal kaglo (*Phalacrocobracs carbosinensis*), paind, and nandi, the last four being migratory birds available only in winter. Larger animals like deer, antelopes, and wild boar have become scarce due to the shrinkage or loss of their habitat, and their hunting is prohibited by law. Nilgai and peacock are held sacred by the Hindus, and hence a Van Vagri will kill them only if he is not likely to be found out doing so. Among domestic animals the Van Vagris eat the goat and buffalo. They eat the flesh of animals killed only by themselves. They never eat carrion as Bhils and Meghwals used to do in the past. Van Vagris also collect honey and even small boys are adept in this activity.

Meat forms a part of the Van Vagri's daily diet. It is usually consumed by roasting it on open fire. When cooked in a pot, only a few spices and salt are added while the fat of the animal or bird serves as the cooking medium.

Among the wild plant foods available in their habitat during various seasons of the year are: tiny seeds of kumat (*Acacia senegal*) (Fig. 13), green pods (*sangri*) of khejri (*Prosopis cineraria*), pea-sized fruit of ker (*Cappais decidua*) (Fig. 14), green, tender pods, kheenpodi of kheenp (*Leptadenia pyrotechinca*), tiny flowers of phog, fruit of jhal (*Salvador oleoides*), fruit of bor (*Zizyphus jujuba*), karela (a small, oval-shaped fruit growing on a creeper), green pods, *patdi* of baund/babul (*Acacia arabica nilotica*), fruit of gol kakdi (a variety of cucumber), and kankhera (a small fruit that grows on a creeper). Several of these foods are astringent and require elaborate processing before they can be consumed. The Van Vagris usually do not have patience for this, and hence they eat these foods only occasionally. The principal source of the vegetable component of their diet is cooked food begged by their women from the homes of upper caste Hindu peasants in the villages. This consists of roti (unleavened bread) of bajra (*Pennisetum typhoides*), *dal* (pulses) of *moth* (*Phaseolus aconitifolius*), urad (*Vigna mungo*), and *mung* (*Vigna radiatus*), curry of guar (*Cymopsis tetragonolobus*), and *raabdi* (gruel of bajra flour cooked in butter milk). The peasantry in Rajasthan have a strong sense of piety and a beggar is never turned away empty-handed from a farmer's home.

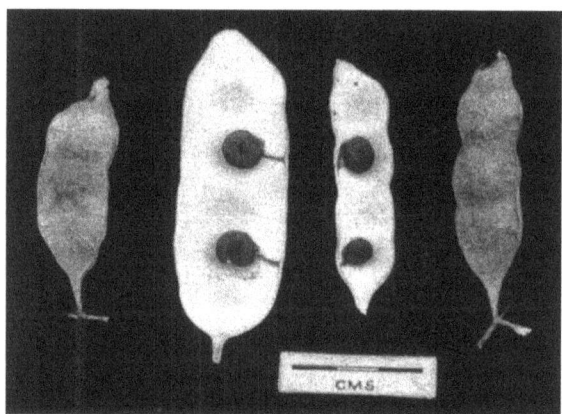

Fig. 13. *Kumat* pods and seeds

Fig. 14. Girs collecting *Ker* fruit

A part of the game hunted by the Van Vagris as also the honey collected by them is sold to local farmers to earn cash which they need to buy clothes, ornaments, utensils, ammunition for guns, and other material items from the market. The Van Vagris make *idundis* (headrests) of *munj* (*Saccrum munja*) grass which are sold for use by village women. In the past they also used to prepare *sarki* (tents) of *munj* stalks for sale to villagers, but with the easy availability of tarpaulins the demand for these tents is much reduced. Van Vagri males who have been engaged in crop watching for the local peasants are paid in kind after the harvest. The grain so earned by them is sold in the market to earn cash. Except for a few persons who have recently settled down and taken to agriculture, all Van Vagris are landless. They also do not work as labourers on public projects or in private agricultural fields. It is their love for freedom which inhibits them from accepting any job that requires fixed hours of work and externally imposed discipline. On several occasions a number of Van Vagri males accepted Misra's offer of working in his excavation, but none of them ever turned up to work.

The Van Vagris have few material possessions. An average family will have a few aluminium and clay vessels for cooking, eating, drinking and storage of water, their hunting gear, one or two hunting dogs, one or two donkeys to carry their belongings, and a few goats, the last usually kept to be sacrificed to the family goddess on a future occasion. They are indeed very poor and are always complaining about their poverty.

2.9 Hunting Technology and Techniques

The hunting equipment of the Van Vagris consists of following items.

Muzzle-loading gun. This is used to shoot animals as well as birds.

Ranpi/Kuso/Kusi. A wooden staff with a rectangular iron blade hafted at one end. This implement is used to drive out and kill monitor lizards and porcupines from hollows in trees and burrows in the ground. This is similar to the *khanta* of the Kanjars.

Balmo (spear) (Fig. 11). A long (1.5 to 2.0 m) wooden shaft with a long pointed iron blade hafted at the distal end. It is used to hunt a variety of animals.

Kudko (Metal trap) (Fig. 15). The trap is laid in a place frequented by hares, and covered with grass. When the animal enters the trap to eat the grass, a lever is released and the animal is caught in a vice.

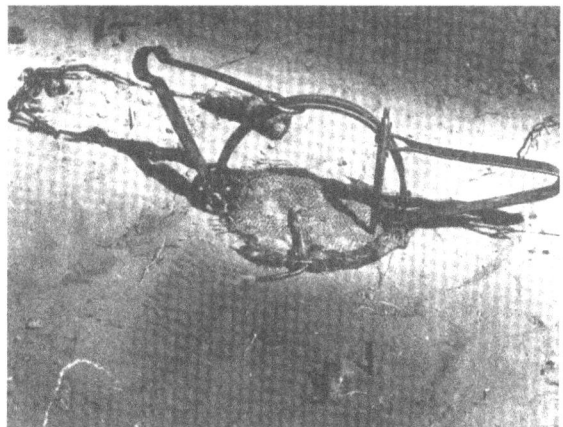

Fig. 15. *Kudko* (Metal Trap) used by the Van Vagris and other hunter-gatherers

Jaal (Net) (Fig. 16). A rectangular net, about 2.1 m long and 1.8 m wide, woven from string and used to trap hares, and partridges, sandgrouse and other birds. It is set in an opening in the thorny fence along the boundary of a field. One side of the net is kept open by raising it above the ground with the support of a stick while the rest of it is held to the ground under the weight of stones. Grains are scattered below the net. When the birds come to feed on the grains, they disturb the stick and the net collapses thereby trapping them.

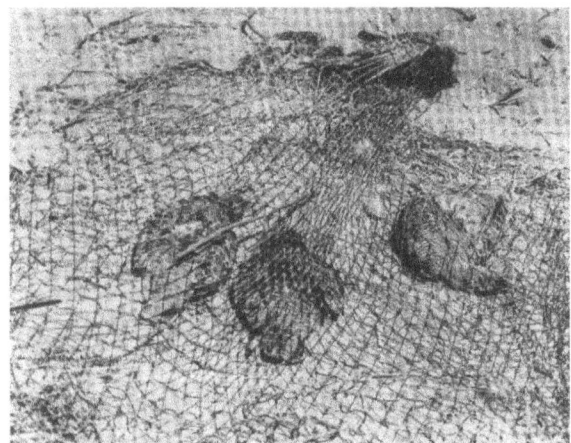

Fig. 16. *Jaal* (Net) with partridges trapped in it

Pansa (Noose trap) (Fig. 17). This consists of 5 to 20 nooses of goat gut, each tied to the upper end of a small stick. All the sticks are held together by a rope. The trap is set in the path of birds by fixing the sticks in the ground and scattering grain near it. When the birds come to eat the grain, they unknowingly pass through the noose, and their weight tightens the noose around their bodies.

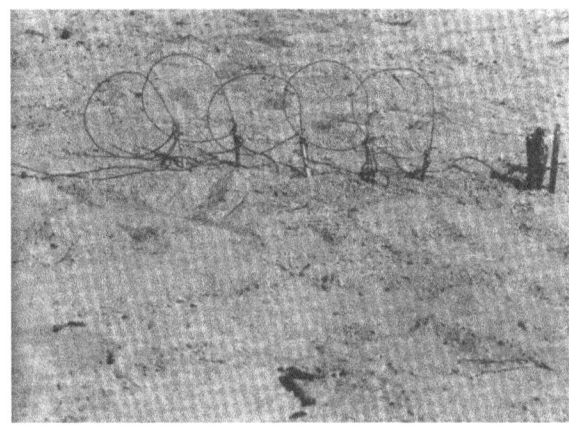

Fig. 17. *Pansa* (Noose Trap)

Dhanudi (Bow) and *Tir* (Arrow) (Fig. 18). The bow is made of *bordi* wood and is about 1.30 m long. The chord is made of copper wire. The shaft of the arrow is made of *munj* stalk and is about 1.40 m long. The head of the arrow, about 20 cm long (excluding the tang), is made of steel, and is either leaf-shaped and flat or cylindrical with a pointed or blunted tip. Both bow and arrow are made by the Van Vagris themselves and are used for shooting animals as well as birds.

Fig. 18. *Dhanudi* (Bow) and *Tir* (Arrows)

The Van Vagris have an intimate knowledge of the habitat and behaviour of the animals and birds that they hunt and they are remarkably efficient hunters and trappers. In a couple of hours two men are able to procure enough game to meet one day's food needs of their families. Misra was witness to their hunting skills on several occasions when accompanying Mohanyo and Samalyo of Baklia camp on their hunting expeditions. The Van Vagris have developed specialized techniques for hunting and trapping different kinds of animals. Their most important hunting aid is their dogs which are slim, agile and extremely efficient in running down hares (Fig. 11). Every family has at least one and usually two or even more dogs which always accompany the hunters during the chase. In olden days the Van Vagris used a tame ox as a decoy while stalking deer and antelopes, but now this practice is no longer in use probably because these animals have become scarce and their hunting is banned. Usually two men hunt together so that the cornering of game can be better managed, and each has company. To trap small animals and birds they fix their nets and traps in an opening in the thorny fence of a field. They then proceed to stir the large heaps of dry branches and twigs of *jhal (Salvadora oleoides)* with a stick to scare away the hares and birds hiding in them. Once the animal or bird starts running or flying, they drive it in the direction of the net or trap. Either their dogs are able to catch the prey or it ends up in the net or trap. Their trained eyes and ears are able to spot partridge and sandgrouse from a considerable distance and they are able to control the path of the movement and flight of the birds by mimicking their sound. A Van Vagri can successfully run down a flock of partridges to fatigue and then trap them or just catch them with his hands. The Van Vagris are also expert shots with guns as well as bows and arrows. Misra once saw Mohanyo drive a lone partridge from one tree to another until finally the bird, perhaps tired, settled down on a *baund/babul (Acacia arabica nilotica)* tree and hid itself in its thick foliage (Fig. 19). Mohanyo circled the tree several times as if to transfix the bird and then shot it with such unerring accuracy that the arrow pierced right through the body of the bird (Fig. 20).

Fig. 19. Partridge shot by Mohanyo in the thick foliage of a *Baund* tree

On another occasion he performed a similar feat with his gun. The Van Vagris sometimes process the birds right after killing or trapping them and roast and consume them on the spot (Fig. 21). They are equally skilled in honey collecting and are not at all afraid of being stung by the bees. Even a ten year old boy with almost no clothing on his body will successfully collect honey from a beehive.

Fig. 20. Partridge with the arrow pierced through its body

Fig. 21. Partridges being dressed by Samalyo

2.10 Religion

The religion of the Van Vagris is centred around the worship of *mata* (mother goddess). Every clan has its own *mata* with a distinct name and a permanent shrine in some town or village where she is also worshipped by Hindu communities. The Van Vagris, however, rarely visit these shrines, and actually worship the goddess only in their camp. Some clans have two or three goddesses, and some goddesses are common to more than one clan. The names of goddesses that Misra was able to ascertain are: Jobner, Shid, Wankal, Karni, Pipli or Piplod, Kalka, Chamunda, and Vigotiya. Essentially the goddess is benevolent but occasionally she can also turn malevolent. She is propitiated to ensure good rain, abundant game and general prosperity, to provide cures from illness, to reveal the identity of evil doers, and to remove the influence of evil spirits.

Fig. 22. Metal box containing the image, dress and ornaments of Bhagu's goddess

The goddess is represented by a metal image which, along with the goddess's clothes, is kept in a cylindrical metal box. When the family is camping, this box is suspended high up in a tree to avoid contact with females and strangers (Fig. 22). When the family is on the move the priest carries the box in his hand and moves away from the rest of the group, again for the same reason. While carrying the goddess the priest must walk and not ride. The image is taken out of the box only on the occasions of worship (*suavani*), which usually takes place during the first nine days (*navrata*) of the dark half of the lunar months of *Asoj* (August-September) and *Chait* (March-April) but it can also be performed on happy occasions like the birth of a child or the recovery of a family member from sickness. On such occasions a goat, dedicated to the goddess in advance, is sacrificed to her, and the cooked flesh is offered to close relatives as *prasad* (food blessed by the goddess).

The priest of the goddess is usually the eldest male member of the family or sometimes of several families of the same lineage. After his death he is generally succeeded by his eldest son, and in case he does not have a son, or the son is not strongly religious, by another male of the family or lineage. The goddess is believed to reveal her preference by taking possession of the would-be successor. The priest has to observe a very strict regimen. He must cook his own food and fetch his own water; he cannot eat food cooked by anyone else, including his wife, mother, sister or daughter. During the *suavani* he must observe strict continence. On this occasion the priest becomes possessed by the goddess who then speaks through him and answers questions asked by the devotees. An important part of the *suavani* ceremony is the *kadhai* (deep frying pan). The priest fries *puris* (wheat cakes) and *gulgula* (balls of sweetened dough) and takes them out of the boiling oil with his hand and not by a ladle. It is believed that because he is under possession by the goddess, his hand will not burn by contact with the boiling oil. This is a belief held not only by the Van Vagris but by members of other communities as well. The Van Vagris live in constant dread of their goddess. Any infringement of the code of conduct prescribed by the goddess will invite her wrath and calamity to the individual and the community. Every care is therefore taken to keep the goddess happy and satisfied so that she maintains a benign attitude to the family and the lineage.

2.11 Relationship with Other Communities

There is very little social interaction between the Van Vagris and other communities (mostly Hindu caste groups) of the area. Since the Van Vagris are largely nomadic and spend most of their time in the *kankar*, they hardly come into contact with the rest of the population. The local people get to see them only from a distance during their movements through the countryside. It is only when Van Vagri women go to the village to sell honey, grass headrests and hunted game or to beg that villagers come in close contact with them. The towns people see them when the Van Vagris occasionally go to the market to purchase items like clothes, utensils, and jewellery. People of those villages where some Van Vagris are employed in crop watching have a better opportunity to observe them. Even in such contexts Van Vagri males remain mostly near the fields and maintain only minimal contact with the villagers. Their shy and meek nature and suspicion of strangers also inhibits contact between them and other people. For this reason members of other communities have only a hazy and stereotyped image of the Van Vagris. When questioned about their opinion about the community they dismiss the latter as an omnivorous, filthy and lazy people not worth bothering about. The Van Vagris do not form part of the Hindu caste system. Their near-omnivorous diet and practice of disposing of their dead by burial (as against cremation among the Hindus) effectively precludes any place for them in the Hindu social system.

Even though the Van Vagris do not form an integral part of the peasant society in the way many artisan and service castes do, they have established a certain degree of symbiosis with the settled population. They supply the meat of wild animals and birds to members of non-vegetarian castes like the Rajputs and Jats, and items like *iduni, sarki* and honey to people of all castes. Many Van Vagri men have established a relationship of *dharambhai* (adopted brother) with one or more peasants and traders. A Van Vagri keeps his money with, and takes loan from, his *dharambhai.* This relationship is one of complete trust between the concerned individuals.

2.12 Relationship with the Politico-Administrative System

Interaction of the Van Vagris with the political and administrative system is virtually non-existent. As the members of the community shun physical labour, they do not come into contact with government contractors undertaking public works like building of roads and railways and digging of tanks and canals. By virtue of their peaceful and law-abiding nature they almost never come into conflict with law enforcing agencies. The unsettled and nomadic lifestyle of the community prevents their children from going to school, and adults from participating in the election process to various elected bodies like village *panchayat*, district council, State assembly and national parliament. The Constitution of India has made provision for special facilities in education and employment to aboriginal communities and former untouchable castes of Hindu society. These groups are officially designated as Scheduled Tribes and Scheduled Castes, respectively, and their names are included in lists drawn up and revised from time to time by the Indian Parliament. Unfortunately, as the very existence of the Van Vagris is unrecognized by the political and administrative system, the community is not included in either of these lists. For this reason the members of this community have completely failed to take advantage of the development facilities they are entitled to.

2.13 Future Prospects

As more and more fallow land is brought under cultivation, the resources for hunting and gathering decline. Since most people in the area are strictly vegetarian, and there is a strong sense of respect for all living things among the general populace, people resent the Van Vagris killing animals and birds in their fields and often abuse them and drive them away. Most farmers also object to Van Vagris even temporarily camping on their land. Coupled with their general poverty, total illiteracy and ignorance of the ways of the world, this kind of treatment adds to the acute sense of misery and self-pity among the Van Vagris. Unfortunately, their economic and social conservatism and the demands of their religion to keep aloof from other people inhibit them from taking to settled life or even working as labourers in fields and on public projects. Misra found only two families settled – one outside Chhapda village, northwest of Jayal town and the other in Sundrasan village, 21 km east of Didwana, and was told of a few other families which have settled down in Budsu and Tosina villages. It will take a long time for all of them to take to settled life whether as cultivators or labourers. In the meantime the degradation of their habitat and depletion of its resources will only make their existence more precarious and miserable.

3. Bhils

The name Bhil is believed by some scholars to be derived from the Dravidian word for bow, which is the characteristic weapon of the tribe, and by others from the root of the Sanskrit verb meaning "to pierce, shoot or kill" in consequence of their proficiency as archers (Erskine 1908: 227). Bhils are one of the major tribal communities of India, numbering over four million people. They are found over a large area covering the whole of Rajasthan, and large parts of Madhya Pradesh, Gujarat and Maharashtra. They are also known to be present in Pakistan in the areas adjoining Rajasthan. Their main concentration, however, is in the Aravalli hills in southern Rajasthan and the hilly tracts of eastern Gujarat and the adjoining Malwa region of Madhya Pradesh.

Like the other tribes, the Bhils too are divided into a number of clans the number of which differs from one area to the other. Many of their clan names like Bhati, Chauhan, Gehlot, Rathor and Solanki are common to the Rajputs from whom some of the them claim descent. At the beginning of the twentieth century Major K.D. Erskine divided the Bhils into three classes which he denominated the village, the cultivating, and the wild or mountain Bhils. The first consisted of those who have become residents of villages in the plains, usually near the hills, of which they are the watchmen and are incorporated as a portion of the community. The cultivating Bhils were those who have continued their peaceable occupations after their leaders were destroyed or driven by invaders to become desperate plunderers. The third class, that of the wild or mountain Bhil, "comprises all that part of the tribe which, preferring savage freedom and indolence to submission and industry, has continued more or less to subsist by plunder" (Erskine 1908: 229-230). However, today hardly any Bhils live this lawless life. They are all settled and live by peaceful occupations.

In the mountains the Bhils live in *pals* or collections of detached huts, each hut standing on a small knoll in the midst of its patch of cultivated land. The *pals*, which consist sometimes of several hundred huts, cover an immense area and are generally divided into a number of *paras* or *phalas* (hamlets). The various huts are at some distance from each other, and this mode of living, by presenting surprise, gives these people greater security. In the event of an attack by outsiders, one Bhil will beat his drum, and as soon as its sound is heard, other Bhils will follow suit and soon a large number of people will gather to ward off the attack. This pattern of settlement can be seen all through the Aravallis while travelling by road or rail from Udaipur to Ahmedabad.

Most of the Bhils practise agriculture but own only small plots of land. Because of heavy deforestation in recent decades, there has been much soil erosion, and generally the soil in the areas which they inhabit is thin, stony and of poor quality, and there are hardly any irrigation facilities. The yield from their plots is low and most of them live an impoverished life. In addition to cultivation, they work as labourers on the land of prosperous cultivators as well as on public projects or wherever they can find work. All of them engage in hunting wherever game is available. Their principal hunting tool is bow and arrow and they have been reputed archers for ages. In the Mahabharata epic there is a story of a young Bhil, Eklavya, who wanted to learn archery from the reputed teacher, Dronacharya but the latter refused to teach him because of his low social status. Not discouraged, Eklavya made a clay image of Dronacharya, and practised the art in front of it, and became an accomplished archer, even better than Arjuna, Dronacharya's most favourite pupil. As per the tradition, Eklavya went to Drona to pay Gurudakshina, (teacher's fee) to express his gratitude. Peeved that Eklavya was better than Arjuna, Drona asked him to give his right thumb so that he will never be able to draw a bow. Eklavya gladly cut his thumb and handed it over to Drona.

Besides, bow and arrow the Bhils use spear, pellet bow, nets and traps, and trained dogs for hunting (Fig. 23). As big game is now scarce as a consequence of large scale deforestation, they hunt only small game like hare, porcupine, monitor lizard and birds. However, in the olden days, when game was plentiful and the Bhils were living a truly wild life, they were practically omnivorous. Col. James Tod wrote at the beginning of the nineteenth century that the Bhil's stomach "would not revolt at an offal- feeding jackal, a hideous *guana* or half-putrid kine", and according to Erskine, who wrote at the beginning of the last century, "this might be the case even at the present day if the Bhil were actually starving, but not under ordinary circumstances. The tribe is doubtless not very particular as to its food, but there are reported to be certain things which it will not touch , e.g. the flesh of the dog, the Bhil's constant companion in the chase; or of the monkey; or of the alligator, lizard, rat or snake. The Bhils are much addicted to liquor, which is distilled from the flowers of the *mahua (Bassia latifolia)* tree or from the bark of the *babul (Acacia arabica)*. The Bhils who have settled down permanently in villages alongside people of Hindu castes are known as *Gameti* in

Mewar. They too practise hunting occasionally though not much game is now available due to the total disappearance of the forest from the plains.

Fig. 23. Bhils with their dogs and the hares caught by them near 16R locality at Didwana

The wild Bhils were reputed for their truthful nature. If a Bhil committed a crime, even murder, under the influence of liquor, he will confess it in a court of law despite being told by his lawyer not to do so. Their most important deity is Mahadev, and a Bhil will swear by Mahadev, to prove that he is telling the truth. According to a popular legend, once Parvati, asked her consort, Shiva to create a person for her protection during his absence and Shiva created a man from the dirt of his body and this man and his descendants came to be known as Bhils. The legend illustrates the attitude of the upper castes towards the Bhils.

4. Kal Beliyas

The Kal Beliyas are found both in western and eastern parts of the State. Their main occupation is catching snakes and entertaining people by displaying them and making them sway to the tune of music from their flute (*been*) made of gourd. They also hunt small game and trap birds and sell them to village people. They hunt with the help of dogs of which every family has one or more. The Kal Beliyas are almost completely nomadic and can often be seen moving in groups of several families with their meagre belongings loaded on donkeys and sometimes on carts pulled by donkeys (Fig. 24). Their women entertain people by song and dance, and reportedly, at least some of them, also indulge in prostitution. Some of the women are excellent dancers, and one of them, Gulabo earned national fame for her extraordinary proficiency in this art, and was even sent abroad to perform in some of the Festivals of India which are regularly organized by the Indian Government in foreign countries, particularly those of Europe, the United States, and Japan. The Kal Beliya dancers also take part in the cultural festivals organized by the Western Zone Cultural Centre at Udaipur. In fact, this Centre has done a lot to promote Kal Beliya dancing.

Fig. 24. A group of Kal Beliyas on the move through Balathal village

Some of the Kal Beliyas have been settled by the Government in exclusive colonies in recent decades. One such colony is located about three km. east of the Karanpur village which is situated between the Udaipur airport at Dabok and Vallabhnagar town. The colony is located on barren, treeless and rocky land and there is no other habitation in the immediate vicinity. We visited the colony on two occasions and interviewed the inhabitants. Most of them, not only children but also adult males and females, were suffering from severe skin disease, apparently due to unhygienic living condition and lack of regular bathing, and they entreated us for some medicine for its cure. The women from the colony go to the nearby villages for begging and for entertaining the people by their music and dance.

There is an open-air shrine of the Kal Beliya goddess in the colony. The goddess is represented by terracotta images and is dressed in very colourful clothes. Another deity of the Kal Beliyas is Rada Deo which is also worshipped by some of the lower Hindu castes. A shrine of the deity exists on the stone and mud embankment along the eastern edge of the large depression between Puriakheri and Balathal villages in Udaipur district. Here the Kal Beliyas from the nearby areas come on special occasions to worship the deity who is represented by an undressed stone slab. They offer meat and liquor to the deity, and sing songs in his praise. We witnessed the worship in the month of February 2000. Almost all the Kal Beliya men and women present on the occasion were heavily drunk, and were squabbling among themselves.

Other communities in Rajasthan which practise hunting though not regularly are Meghwals, a scheduled caste, most probably derived from the Bhils, Aheriyas, Bagris, Bawarias, and Sansis /Sansiyas, but not much information is available on them. All of them also indulge in theft and other crimes. Some of the Sansiyas have been settled in a colony some three km. away from Bagor village in Bhilwara district to wean them away from crime but not all of them have given up criminal activities. Their women are also very daring and manage the affairs of the family while their men are in prison.

CENTRAL INDIA

Geographical Setting

Central India can be broadly defined as the area delimited by the Ganga plains in the north, Aravalli hills in the west, Chota Nagpur plateau in the east, and the Tapi river in the south. Two major hill ranges, namely the Vindhyas and the Satpuras, occupy its northern and southern portion, and Deccan traps of the Sahyadri hills are found in the west. Several perennial rivers like the Chambal, Son, Mahanadi and Narmada and their large tributary networks drain the region. Central India receives ample rainfall which ranges from about 800 mm in the west to around 2000 mm in the east. The hills and valleys are covered by a dense dry deciduous woodland. The forests abound in an immense variety of plant foods and an almost equally rich variety of herbivores. The Vindhya hills, formed of sandstone, contain several thousand naturally formed rockshelters. The region thus has all the resources – water, food and shelter – in ample measure to support human populations. That the faunal wealth was equally rich in the past is shown by the impressive fossil record of the Yamuna, Son, Belan, Adwa and Narmada valleys. The region also shelters the largest concentration of tribal population in the country. Though almost all of them practise agriculture, they also combine it with varying degrees of hunting and gathering.

It is therefore no surprise that the region has continuously supported human populations right from the Lower Palaeolithic times. A large number of prehistoric sites of different stages have been discovered in different parts of the region, and a number of them like Sihawal, Patpara, Baghor, and Khetaunhi in the Son valley, and Adamgarh, Bhimbetka and Samnapur in the Narmada valley have been excavated. They have provided rich evidence of stone age occupation in the form of stone tools, faunal remains, and in the case of the Mesolithic period, human skeletal remains. The rockshelters contain an extraordinary wealth of paintings in red, white and green colours, which depict scenes of wild animals, hunting, fishing, plant food gathering, honey collecting and of social and religious life (Fig. 25).

Agriculture-based life appeared in the region in the third millennium B.C. and flourished mainly in the fertile river valleys of the Malwa plateau. The forested hills were not very suitable for agriculture and therefore hunter-gatherers continued to maintain their traditional lifestyle in them. Even to this day there are a number of groups which live to a considerable extent by hunting-gathering. We have studied two of them, namely the Pardhis and Kuchbandhias, in the field, and are presenting brief accounts of their lifeways below.

Pardhis

The word Pardhi is derived from the Sanskrit *paradh*, meaning hunt or hunting. One of their groups is known as 'Adivichanchar'. This word is derived from the Sanskrit *atavi* meaning forest and *sanchar* meaning wanderer, that is wanderer of the forest. The other names used for the whole or a section of the community are: Shikari, Bahelia, Moghia, Mirshikar, Phans or Phanse Pardhi and Takankar. Shikari, the common Indian name for a hunter, is particularly applied to those who use firearms, which most Pardhis refuse to do. Moghia is the Hindi word for fowler, and Takankar is the name of a small occupational offshoot in Vidarbha, who travel from village to village and roughen the household stone grinding mills when they have worn smooth. The word Takankar is derived from *takna*, meaning to tap or chisel. The connotation of hunting associated with almost all the names of the community clearly shows that the principal traditional occupation of the community is hunting.

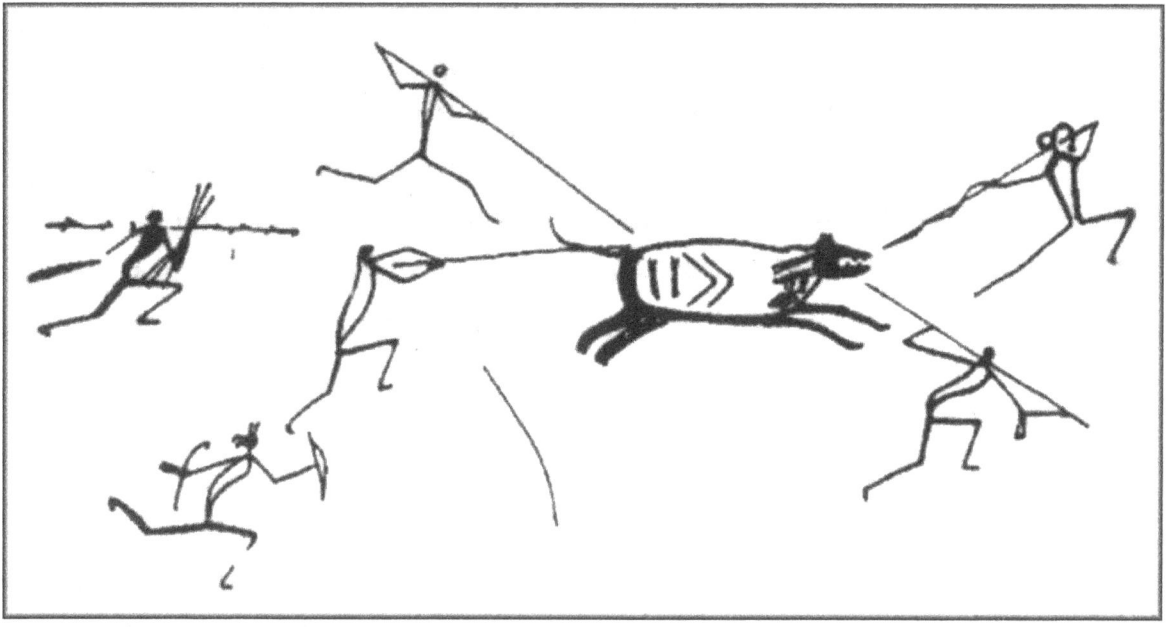

Fig. 25. A hunting scene from the prehistoric rock paintings at Bhimbetka, Sehore distraict, Madhya Pradesh

Sources of Information

The information presented in this chapter is based on two sources.

1. Field-work carried out by me and V.N. Misra, among the Pardhis of Chandarpura and Umrari villages in Sagar District, and in Aanvaria village and a temporary camp near Samnapur village, in Narsinghpur District, in Madhya Pradesh. The field-work was done while V.N. Misra and S.N. Rajaguru were excavating a Palaeolithic site at Samnapur (23° 06′ 17″ N : 79° 07′ 30″) on the Narmada River. Pardhi informants were interviewed and the behaviour of members of the community was observed in their seasonal settlements and temporary camps.

2. From previously published brief accounts and passing references to the community (Sherring 1879: 202; Russell and Hira Lal 1916 III: 159-171; Enthoven 1922 III: 169-174; Sangave 1967: 81-88; Shah 1968: 37; Mathur 1969; Maharashtra Census Office 1972: 177-182; Malhotra *et al.* 1983: 21-39), particularly those written by R.V. Russell and R,B. Hira Lal, and R.E. Enthoven.

The accounts of Enthoven and Russell and Hira Lal are sometimes contradictory and cannot be fully relied upon because they are based on information collected by government functionaries. They are, however, useful for providing a historical perspective and for visualizing the degree of change in the community over the last several decades.

Like most of the other hunting communities living in the vicinity of settled villages and towns and in an environment largely depleted of wild game, the Pardhis too are engaged in crime as an alternative source of livelihood. For this reason they are extremely suspicious and distrustful of strangers, and are very reluctant to part with personal information like their own and their parents' names, the place of their residence, hunting activities, and resent being photographed. They are afraid that the person collecting the information may pass it on to the police and this may lead to their harassment and even arrest for some crime they may or may not have committed. However, once they are satisfied with the identity and intentions of the interviewer, they are quite cooperative and even enthusiastic in providing information. We found most of our Pardhi informants – both men and women – extremely cooperative and patient. They not only answered whatever questions we asked, but also permitted us to take photographs and very patiently demonstrated the use of the various items of their hunting equipment. They even agreed to sell us, after some persuasion, a few of the items. They never asked for any money in return for providing information and willingly accepted what we gave them. This behaviour was in sharp contrast to that of several other communities with whom we have worked.

On only one occasion did we face a problem. In the Samnapur forest camp, Motilal, a young boy of 16-18 years, refused to permit us to take photographs of the camp (*dera*). He was deeply suspicious of our motives. He repeatedly threatened to pack up and leave and angrily pleaded with other members of the camp to bring their bullocks and pack up. When he found that others were reluctant to heed his pleas, he brought his own two bullocks and started packing his things. We tried our best to convince him that we meant no harm to him and his relatives but he would not relent. Even his father, Rameshwar, and uncle, Raju and others who were initially agreeable to our taking pictures were finally converted to Motilal's thinking and refused us permission. They all said that they had never had such an experience (i.e. of strangers asking them questions about their genealogy, occupation, etc. and wishing to take pictures). Motilal offered to take the whole group with their belongings to the Suatala Police Station and permit us to take photographs there. After listening to other members of the camp, it transpired that some years ago there was an incident of theft and a large number of Pardhis were arrested by the Police and photographed. They feared that we were taking their pictures for their eventual arrest. Finally, we told them that we would not take any pictures and that they need not move their camp for fear of us.

Settlements and Camps

From our informants we gathered the names of a number of Pardhi settlements, mainly in Sagar District of Madhya Pradesh. These are:

Jamunia, near Gotegaon (23° 14'N : 79° 04'E)
Sale Chowk near Sagar railway station (23° 51'N : 78° 45'E)
Sahawan
Dahalwara, beyond the railway crossing at Gadarwara (22° 56'N : 78° 48'E)
Baranjh
Singpur-Gajanpur, 10 km southeast of Deori (23° 26'N : 79° 07'E)
Ghugad-Baroda near Sagar town (23° 43'N : 78° 42'E)
Chandarpura (23° 47'N : 78° 56'E)
Umrari (23° 36'N : 78° 52'E)

Tal Chidi near Lidhaura, 16 km from Surki
(23° 46'N : 78° 46'E)
Ishwarpur near Bina Bara
Bakswar in Chhatarpur district

Most of these settlements are in Sagar District. We were not told about any settlements in Narsinghpur District although we came across one temporary camp and met one group which was on the move. At Samnapur the local people told us that the Pardhis come there during the winter season from Sagar and Damoh. They keep goats and poultry. The men hunt with dogs and sell medicines for wounds and eczema, etc., while their women sell cheap jewellery, cosmetics, combs, mirrors, etc.

We visited the settlements of Chandarpura, Umrari and Aanvaria, and a temporary camp in the forest, by the side of the Narsinghpur-Jabalpur highway, near Samnapur village, on the northern bank of the Narmada River in Narsinghpur District.
A brief description of these settlements and camps is given below.

A. Chandarpura (Fig. 26)

This is an exclusively Pardhi settlement, located about 2 km east of the Narsinghpur-Sagar road and about 65 km north of the small market place of Premnagar at the crossing of Narsinghpur-Sagar and Jabalpur-Bhopal highways (*Rajmarg*). Founded about 50 years ago, the settlement is situated at the foot of a low hillock on rocky land. Today only patches of a highly degraded forest survive in the immediate vicinity of the settlement but both large game like sambar, chital and wild boar and small game like fox, jackal, hare and porcupine as well as a variety of birds are available in it. Some decades ago, the forest certainly was more extensive and dense and the wild plant food resources far more plentiful. That must have been the major attraction for founding the settlement.

Fig. 26. Pardhi settlement at Chandarpura village

The settlement consists of the following 22 individuals and their families

1. Lakhan, 2. Palangchand, 3. Lotu, 4. Balai, 5. Dubraj, 6. Sukal, 7. Kariya, 8. Bishanchand, 9. Pojam, 10. Omkar, 11. Dukhichand, 12. Bundel, 13. Badebhai, 14. Bade, 15. Mundobai, 16. Roslal, 17. Topilal, 18. Badde, 19. Doslal alias Jhansiwala, 20. Kherchand, 21. Kanjri, 22. Manohar.

Of these, only Bishanchand, Pojam, Palangchand, Lakhanchand, Manohar, Badebhai, Kariya, Doslal and Topilal were actually present in Chandarpura at the time of our visit. The rest were away for *manihari* (selling bangles, cheap jewellery and cosmetics) business.

All the residents of the settlement are related to each other by blood or marriage. The first twelve individuals are related by blood and belong to the Jhalawar or Jhadewalia clan and to the lineage of Chandan Singh, Chandan Singh's son, Jujhar Singh had nine sons but the children of only three of them, namely Pittal Singh, Sanwal Singh, and Phullu live in this settlement, Lakhanchand alias Pavan,

Palangchand, Lotu, Balai, Dubraj, Sukal and Kariya are the sons of Pittal Singh. Pojam is the son of Sanwal Singh, and Omkar, Dukhichand and Bundel are the sons of Phullu. Geslal, Doslal, Roslal, Topilal and Bade are sons-in-law of Pittal Singh. Geslal is married to Ashabai, Doslal to Palangbai, Roslal to Guddi, Topilal to Halkibai and Bade to Jalbai, Bishanchand also belongs to the Chandan Singh lineage. Kanjri is a daughter of Pittal Singh and is almost certainly the wife of one of the non-Jhalawar clan males of the settlement. Kherchand, Badde and Manohar too are related to Jhalawar clan by marriage to their women. Similarly, Mundobai is almost certainly a wife of one of the Jhalawar men.

B. Umrari

This is a small village about 2 km south of Chandarpura and is located on both sides of the Narsinghpur-Sagar road. There are only a few Pardhi families which live separately from other castes on the eastern side of the road. These families belong to the five sons of Sanwal Singh (Umarchand, Lagharchand, Phatphat, Lotus and Shoukeen). Originally they were living in Chandarpura with their cousins but shifted to Umrari 10 or 12 years ago. Another family is that of Geslal who is married to Ashabai, one of the daughters of the late Pittal Singh of Chandarpura settlement. There are several families of Kuchbandhias, another hunting-gathering community of the region, in this village, and there is considerable interaction between them and the Pardhis in hunting activities and social life.

C. Aanvaria

Located 7 km north of Premnagar crossing along the western edge of the Narsinghpur-Sagar road is the small hamlet of Aanvaria. There are only two Pardhi families here and they live a little away from the other castes in the village. These families belong to Bhagirath's paternal and maternal uncles. We did not, however, have an opportunity to meet either of them. At the time of our visit to this hamlet, Bhagirath, along with his mother, Ramkali, three brothers, wife and a female child, was temporarily living with his maternal uncle and was planning to move to another place in search of a living. Bhagirath's father, Mokal, lives in Ishwarpur village near Bina Bara with his second wife.

D. Forest Camp near Samnapur

This camp primarily consists of people of the Jhalawar clan and Chandan Singh's lineage. Six of the families here belong to the sons of Satal, a grandson of Chandan Singh. They are Rameshwar, Ramphal, Sukke, Badri, Indurchand and Raju, born from Satal's two wives, Satal lived in Jamunia village and four of his sons – Sukke, Badri, Indurchand and Raju – also live there while the other two, Rameshwar and Ramphal, live in Gotegaon and Kuiya near Jhira Ghat, respectively. The three other families in the camp are of men who are married to daughters of Satal. They are:

Pardeshi, husband of Rameshwar's sister, Kosambai.

Shivram, son of Ramesh and Kamlabai. Ramesh lived in Nayakhera. After his death Kamlabai came back to live with her parents in Jamunia.

Jumman, son of Babu and Sakkaria. Babu died of tuberculosis and his wife started living with a man of the Baraua caste in Sagar. Jumman was brought up by his maternal grandmother and is now living with his maternal uncle.

Most of the Pardhis in these settlements and temporary camps belong to the Bail Pardhi section of the community, to the Jhalawar *kuri* or *kuli* (clan) and a single lineage. They are descended from a common ancestor, namely Chandan Singh.

Informants

Our data came from a large number of informants in the following villages and camp, and the chief among them were:

Vakilchand, son of Kanchhedi, village Jamunia, District Narsinghpur.

Bhagirath, son of Mokal, village Jamunia, District Narsinghpur.

Pardeshi, son of Pitam Singh, Shivram, son of Ramesh, and Jumman, son of Babu, village Jamunia, District Narsinghpur.

Rameshwar and Raju, sons of Satal, village Jamunia, District Narsinghpur.
Palangchand, Bishanchand and Nandlal alias Badde, sons of Pittal Singh, village Chandarpura, District Sagar.

Geslal, son of Sarabji and Munna, son of Paramlal, village Umrari, District Sagar.

We met Vakilchand 8 km south of Jhira Ghat (on the Narsinghpur-Sagar Road) while he, along with other members of his group, was returning home from a 15 day trading trip to the annual Burman Ghat fair on the Narmada River. We met Bhagirath and his mother and wife the same day at his home in Aanvaria hamlet. We interviewed Palangchand, Bishanchand, Nandlal alias Badde and several others of Chandarpura village. We visited the forest camp near Samnapur and talked to Rameshwar, Raju, Pardeshi, Shivram and Jumman and other members of the camp. We visited Umrari village, spoke to Geslal, Munna and others and watched a demonstration of various items of hunting equipment. We also bought some of them.

Distribution and Population

The Pardhis are found in Maharashtra, Madhya Pradesh (M.P.), Gujarat and Karnataka. In Madhya Pradesh they are designated both as a Scheduled Tribe and a Scheduled Caste. In the other three States they are designated only as a Scheduled Tribe.

According to the 1961 Census, their total population was only 28,178, distributed in these four States as follows:

Maharashtra	21,417
Madhya Pradesh	5,946
Gujarat	456
Karnataka	344

In addition there is a community in Kachchh known as Paradhi which is thought to be the same as Pardhi (Shah 1968: 37). Their population in 1961 was 2,846.

In 1901 the population of the community in the Bombay Presidency, where it is largely found, was 12,214 of which nearly half (5,150) were found in Khandesh alone and the only other places in which they were numerous were Kachchh State and Nasik, Sholapur and Bijapur districts. These figures show a very slow increase in their population over sixty years.

Population figures as available from census records cannot be relied upon in the case of nomadic communities like the Pardhis. The census enumeration which takes place every ten years is carried out by Government employees who are temporarily drafted for this work. They go to individual houses in localities assigned to them on a fixed day to carry out the enumeration. It is unrealistic to expect them to chase nomads in the forests and the bush away from permanent settlements. For us it was not possible to collect any significant data on population and fertility during short spells of fieldwork, more so because our major interest was in collecting information on hunting and gathering strategies and techniques, and settlement patterns. Even so we managed to collect a limited amount of genealogical data which we give below. It might give some idea of fertility and growth of population in the community.

Most of the residents of these settlements and inmates of the camps belong to the Bail (bull) Pardhi group of the Pardhi community, and to a single clan, namely Jhalawar or Jhadewalia, and to a single lineage, namely that of Chandan Singh. Other members of these settlements and camps are related to members of the lineage through marriage.

Genealogy of *Chandan Singh

* = Deceased; M = male; F = female; = = married to

Chandan Singh lived in Tal Chidi near Lidhaura, 16 km from Surki, close to Sagar town. The name of only one of his children, namely Jujhar Singh, is remembered.

*Jujhar Singh

Jujhar Singh had nine sons from four wives but information was available only about four sons. They are:

1. *Pittal Singh, 2. Sanwal Singh, 3. *Phullu, 4.*Satal

Pittal Singh seems to have been a man of uncommon courage and leadership. He is highly venerated by his descendants who proudly speak of his exploits and show his framed portrait to visitors. He had six wives of whom four are alive. As and when his brothers died, he married their wives. He had nineteen children – twelve sons and seven daughters. Their names are as follows.

*Pittal Singh

1. M Harakchand*, 2. M Hukam, 3. M Daulat, 4. M Lakhan alias Pavan, 5. M Palangchand, 6. M Lotu, 7. M Balai, 8. M Dubraj, 9. M Halke, 10. M Sukal, 11. M Kariya, 12. F Parambai, 13. F Ashabai = M Geslal, 14. F Palangbai = M Doslal, 15. F Bhadra, 16. M Kanjri, 17. F Guddi = M Roslal, 18. F Halkibai = M Topilal, 19. F Jalbai = M Bade

Sanwal Singh

He has following six sons.

M Umarchand, 2. M Lagharchand, 3. M Phatphat, 4. M Lotus, 5. M Shoukeen, and 6. M Pojam

*Satal

Satal has six sons and eight daughters with the following names.

1. M Rameshwar, 2. M Ramphal, 3. M Sukke, 4. M Badri, 5. M Indurchand, 6. M Raju, 7. F Kosambai = M Pardeshi, 8. F Narbadi, 9. F Sakkaria = M Babu, 10. F Kamlabai = M Babu, 11. F Pentbai, 12. F Munnabai, 13. F Dropadibai, 14. F Jijja

*Phullu

Phullu has three sons and one daughter.

M Omkar, 2. M Dukhichand, 3. M Bundel, and 4. F Rajbanti

Besides, the names of the children of Kanchhedi of Jamunia village, near Gotegaon were given to us by Vakilchand, one of his sons whom we met by chance but found very cooperative in providing information.

*Kanchhedi

Kanchedi has four sons and five daughters.

1. F Vakilbai, 2. M Vakil, 3. F Prabha, 4. M Garibchand, 5. F Chenpu, 6. M Tandu, 7. F Noni, 8. M Khoda, 9. F Anita

The above details show that the Pardhis have a very high fertility rate.

Settlement Pattern

Until the early part of the last century the Pardhis were a totally nomadic people. According to Enthoven (1922: 172), "During fair weather Pardhis wander from place to place in bands of three to six families. The men walk ahead carrying nets and baskets, followed by the women with the wooden cots and mat huts, and children carrying earthen pots and pans. Occasionally, they own a bullock or buffalo, on which are loaded blankets, baskets, bamboo sticks, nets and mats. The long rack-like frames in which they fit the delicate horse-hair nooses are most skillfully made, and do great damage to the game. While on the move, they live outside of villages under bamboo frames covered with matting, or under the shade of trees. Their huts are seven feet by four and five feet high, with walls and slanting roofs of straw matting, which they roll up and carry off in a few moments. If overtaken by rain, they take shelter in the nearest village".

Today, however, they are semi-nomadic people. They have a permanent home base away from peasant villages where they live during the rainy season. Here they maintain small rectangular huts made of stone, brick or mud-brick walls with a thatched or tiled roof. Occasionally the hut is circular with a conical thatched roof. During the eight dry months of the year they are on the move and only the old people stay on at the home base. During their wanderings they camp in the forest, away from villages and towns, either in the open or in small, flimsy huts. Made of tree branches, leaves, old cloth, plastic or tarpaulin, these huts can be raised in a few hours and abandoned without dismantling. Camping in the forest is convenient for their hunting operations and also keeps them out of sight of the police. The huts are used mainly for keeping their limited belongings and for providing shelter to small children from the sun and rain. Most of their activities like cooking, eating and sleeping take place in the open. The men and grown up boys engage in hunting while the women go to the villages to sell bangles and cosmetics to peasant women. These temporary camps consist of five to ten families which are related to each other by blood or marriage. In a typical camp there will be families of two or three brothers and their brothers-in-law. The camps are moved every few weeks after the game in the forest and the scope for trade in the nearby villages have been fully exploited. While moving camp they carry their goods either on bullocks or in bullock carts. The use of horses and donkeys is banned by tradition. At the approach of the monsoon they return to their permanent home base and repair the huts. Those who have land come back to their settlement for two or three weeks during winter to harvest the crops. For example, during our visit to Umrari village, Paramlal, his wife and children were away trading and were expected back after 15 days to harvest their crops.

We were able to observe one temporary camp in a forest clearing near the village of Samnapur. In this camp there were ten families but only five huts, each one belonging to only one family. The other families were camping in the open. Each family had at least 4-5 goats, and some had 15-20 of them and also a few fowls. Some of them also had bullocks and at least one family had a bullock cart. This camp had been here for over a month. It had shifted to Khomna for eight days but came back because there was better game (specially wild boar) in the forest here.

Composition of the Settlements and Camps

The composition of a permanent settlement or a temporary camp (*dera*) is determined entirely by kinship ties – both consanguineal and affinal. Persons not related by kinship ties to some member of the settlement or camp cannot find a place in it. A typical camp will consist of the families of two or more brothers and of their brothers-in-law. Besides, other consanguineal and affinal relations like parents, nephews, sisters and their husbands may also form a part of it. As in other hunting-gathering communities, there is a particularly close bond between a man and his wife's brother and they and their families invariably share a common camp. This principle can be clearly seen in the composition of the settlements and camps described above.

The composition of both permanent settlements and temporary camps is very unstable and members frequently shift their residence from one settlement or camp to another for a variety of reasons. These include quarrels among brothers over property (mainly land), search for security through proximity to relatives, escape from harassment by members of the group or of another community and the search for better living conditions. Many such examples are available in the data collected by us. For example, Sanwal Singh left Chandarpura because of a quarrel with his brothers. The two families in the Umrari settlement – one of Geslal and the other of Paramlal, brother of Geslal's wife – first moved from Chandarpura to Koania, 10 km southwest of Umrari and then, after only one year's stay in Koania, they shifted to Umrari. Paramlal purchased two acres of land for Rs. 9,000, from Kherchand, who had received it as *patta* (allotment by the Government). Jujhar Singh lived in Tal Chidi, south of Sagar where he had land but he was harassed by the people of other castes. After his death, his son, Sanwal Singh, was also harassed by the villagers and so he came to Chandarpura and bought land there. Similarly, the two Pardhi families in Jamunia had shifted from Madparia, 4 km from Jamunia, about 15 years ago and purchased land in Gotegaon and Jamunia. Satal also shifted from Tal Chidi to Medwasa (Chandarpura) but quarreled with his brothers there. His brother Pittal Singh took away the land. Satal then shifted to his father-in-law's village, Bina in Deori Tehsil and from there to Madparia after he had a quarrel with his in-laws. Finally, he went to Jamunia and bought land there about 25 years ago and since then he and his family have lived there.

Language

The Pardhis normally speak the language of the State in which they live. Most of them, however, are able to speak Gujarati which suggests that they have migrated to other States from Gujarat at some stage in the not too distant past. The Pardhis of Madhya Pradesh from whom we collected our data normally speak Hindi but many of them can also speak Gujarati. It is, however, intriguing that they are totally absent in the western districts of Madhya Pradesh which are contiguous to Gujarat and where they should be expected if the hypothesis of their migration from Gujarat is valid. The Madhya Pradesh Pardhis are also said to know Marathi and Urdu and those in Karnataka speak Kannada.

Dress and Appearance (Figs. 27-28)

According to Russell and Hira Lal (1916: 363), "In dress and appearance the Pardhis are disreputable and dirty. Their features are dark and their hair matted and unkempt. They never wear shoes and say that they are protected by a special promise of the goddess Devi to their first ancestor that no insect or reptile in the forest should injure them. The truth no doubt, is, that shoes would make it impossible for them to approach their game without disturbing it, and from long practice of walking bare foot the soles of their feet become impervious to thorns and minor injuries. Their women do not have their nose pierced and never wear spangles or other marks on the forehead." However, we found many of the Pardhi men and women tall, fair and handsome. Their habits of cleanliness have also changed over the decades. Many of them are now cleanly dressed and well groomed and are conscious of being seen as respectable members of society. There is little difference in the dress of Pardhi males and females and that of members of the other communities.

Social Organisation

As a collection of wandering bands of hunters and game snarers, the Pardhis have always offered asylum to individual outcasts or splinter groups of other tribes or castes. It is therefore a somewhat heterogeneous group, recruited from

Fig. 27. A Pardhi woman at Chandarpura village with a cloth bundle containing bangles and other items for sale

Fig. 28. Pardhi men at Chandarpura village

various communities like the Rajputs, Kolis, Vaghris, Dhangars, Kabbligars and Korchars. For this reason, the social customs of the tribe tend to vary from place to place. According to their legends their first ancestor was a Gond to whom Mahadeo taught the art of snaring game so that he might avoid the sin of shooting it.

The Pardhis are usually considered an impure caste, whose touch is a defilement to Hindus. According to Russell and Hira Lal (1916), in central India Brahmins do not officiate at their ceremonies, but according to Enthoven (1922), in western India they do. However, the Pardhis consult the village *joshi* or astrologer to determine a propitious date for marriage. They have to pay for such services in money, as Brahmins usually refuse to accept even uncooked grain from them. Pardhis consider Kuchbandhias, another hunting-gathering community in central India, as inferior to them because the latter eat food from all communities. The Pardhis do not eat food from the Kuchbandhias.

The tribe is divided into a number of endogamous groups but not all of them are found in every region. According to various writers on the community, the following groups are known among them:

1. Shikari or Bhil Pardhis (who use firearms); 2. Phanse Pardhis (who hunt with traps and snares); 3. Langoti Pardhis (so called because they wear only a narrow strip of cloth round their loins); 4. Takankars (who roughen household grinding mills); 5. Chita Pardhis or Chitewale (who hunt with a tame leopard); 6. Bail Pardhis or Gayake (who stalk their prey behind a bullock); 7. Gosain Pardhis (who dress like religious mendicants in ochre-coloured clothes and do not kill deer but only hares, jackals and foxes); 8. Shishi ke Telwale (who sell crocodile oil); 9. Bandarwale (who go about with performing monkeys); 10. Hiran Pardhis (who hunt deer); 11. Adivichanchar; 12. Mir; 13. Korchar and 14. Vaghri.

According to Enthoven, in central India the Bahelias and Pardhis merge into one another and are not recognisable as distinct groups. The Bahelias have a sub-caste known as Karijat, the members of which only kill birds of a black colour.

According to Enthoven (1922), the bulk of the tribe is divided into totemistic divisions worshipping different deities or *devaks*, of which the principal are:

Thorns of the *arai* shrub (*Mimosa rubricaulis*)
Thorns of the *bor* tree (*Zizyphus jujuba*)
Leaves of the shami tree (*Prosopis spicigera*)
Mango (*Mangifera indica*)
Jambhul (*Eugenia jambolana*)
Umbar (*Ficus glomerata*)

Intermarriage among members of clans having the same *devak* is prohibited. Similarly, members of a clan will not consume an animal or plant which is their totem. For example, the people of Rameshwar's *kuri* do not eat *khara* (hare) since they regard it as their ancestor nor do they eat *jam* (*Eugenia jambolana*), *thulla* and *kutkana*. The people of Shivram's clan do not eat *kumhda* (pumpkin).

The Pardhis have a clan *panchayat* and a headman called *naik* or leader, both of whom command considerable authority. The *panchayat* resolves social disputes and takes decisions on matters affecting the clan. At the *panchayat* meetings, known as Deokaria or 'An act performed in honour of God', arrangements for expeditions are discussed and caste disputes resolved. The penalty for social offences is a fine of a specified quantity of liquor, the liquor provided by male and female delinquents being drunk by the men and women respectively. The punishment for adultery in either sex used to consist of cutting off a piece of the left ear with a razor, and a man guilty of intercourse with a prostitute was punished as if he had committed adultery. But it is doubtful that this strong code of conduct is enforced today. The Pardhi women are said to be virtuous.

Early accounts of the community (Russell and Hira Lal 1916; Enthoven 1922) show that they practised the primitive method of trial by ordeal. If a person of either sex was suspected of misconduct like adultery or similar serious offence, he or she was made to pick a coin out of a jar of boiling oil. If the coin was picked out without harming the hand, the person was declared innocent. If he/she refused to do this, or if the hand was burnt, the person was declared guilty. A woman found guilty in this manner was turned out of the caste. In the case of females, another method was to put a *pipal* leaf on her hand and a red-hot axe over that. If her hand was burnt or if she refused to stand the test she was pronounced guilty. Or, in the case of a man, the accused was made to dive into water, and as he dived an arrow was shot from a bow. A swift runner fetched and brought back the arrow, and if the diver could remain under water until the runner had returned he was held to be innocent. In Nimar, if an unmarried girl became pregnant, two cakes of dough were prepared, a piece of silver being placed in one and a lump of coal in the other. The girl took one of the cakes, and if it was found to contain the coal she was expelled from the community, while if she chose the piece of silver she was pardoned and made over to one of the caste. The idea of the ordeal was apparently to decide the question of whether her condition was caused by a Pardhi or an outsider.

Family and Marriage

The typical Pardhi family is of the nuclear type consisting of a man, his wife and unmarried children. As soon as the sons get married, they set up their own families, and the daughters go to live with their husbands. It is stated that members of clans bearing Rajput names will take daughters from other clans in marriage, but will not give their daughters to them. The people of the Sesodia clan will marry their girls and boys into the Puaanr, Solanki and Pipladia clans. They will accept girls from the Jhalawar clan but will not give their own girls to that clan. There is a definite preference for new marriage alliances into a clan where already previous marriages have taken place. For example, of the six sons of Satal, three, namely Sukke, Badri and Raju, married into the Sesodia clan, two, namely Rameshwar and Indurchand, into the Puaanr clan, and one, Ramphal, into the Solanki clan. Of his daughters, three, namely Pentbai, Dropadibai and Jijja, married into the Solanki clan, three, namely Narbadi, Sakkaria and Kamlabai, married into the Sesodia clan, and two, namely Kosambai and Munnabai, married into the Puaanr clan. Similarly, of the six sons and four daughters of Sanwal Singh, five sons and four daughters married Solanki clan members, and only one son, Umarchand, married into the Malia clan.

The offer of marriage always comes from the boy's parents. Bride price is invariably paid. However, if the boy's parents cannot pay the bride price, then the boy works for three months or so in the bride's house and if the bride's parents approve of him, they marry their daughter to him. Another way to avoid paying bride price is to enter into an exchange marriage whereby the parents of a boy give their daughter in marriage to the brother of the girl who marries their son. Depending on the resources and inclination of the girl's parents, the girls also get a dowry. For example, Rameshwar gave some fifty goats to his daughter, Kosambai, and four goats to his daughter, Kamlabai.

Two brothers may marry two sisters, the elder brother being married to the elder sister and the younger to the younger sister. Polygamy is permitted and practised and a man is allowed to marry two sisters. A man may marry his deceased wife's younger sister. Both divorced women and widows are allowed to remarry. A widow is obliged to marry (*bitha dena*) the younger brother of her husband even if the latter is already married but she cannot marry her cross-cousin. In case a widow has illicit relations with anyone, the man is forced to marry her. If a woman has illicit relations with a man of another community, she elopes with him and is forgotten by her own community. If a girl is seduced by a man of the tribe, she is forcibly married to him by the ceremony of a widow's marriage; but her family would require a bride from her husband's family to compensate for the loss of their girl's honour. According to Enthoven (1922), such a girl can be married only after she has been purified by a Brahmin, and the seducer and the girl's father are fined and made to give a dinner to the caste people. If the seducer belongs to another caste, the girl is allowed to remain in the caste after being purified, and may marry any male of the caste. If the offence is committed several times, the girl is excommunicated. In the case of well-to-do people, child marriages were in vogue, almost certainly in imitation of the practice of higher castes.

Marriages are celebrated all the year around. The ceremony of marriage varies according to the locality in which the tribe resides. Usually the couple walk seven times round a *tanda* or collection of their mat tents. In Vidarbha a cloth is held up by four persons as canopy over them and they are preceded by a married woman carrying five pitchers of water. Some of the elders of the clan act as priests at the marriage ceremony.

According to Enthoven, the Phanse Pardhis differ from the bulk of the Pardhis in some of their social and religious customs. They marry their girls at any age. On the marriage day the bride and bridegroom are decked with chaplets of *pipal* leaves, a tassel of thread hanging over each temple. The skirts of the bride and bridegroom are knotted together seven times, the guests throw red rice over the pair's heads, and the marriage is complete. Polygamy and widow remarriage are allowed and practised.

Disposal of the Dead

Burial is the normal mode of disposing of the dead and the dead are buried within or near the settlement. If a person dies while the group is on the move, he is buried at the place of his death. For example, Vakilchand's sister, Vakilbai, died in camp near Sarsala and was buried there. According to Enthoven, the dead are buried in a horizontal position with the head to the south. In Kachchh, before burial the big toe of the right foot is burnt. Women who die during childbirth and persons who have visited the shrines of their family goddesses are cremated. The bones and ashes of those cremated are consigned to water. Unlike most Hindus, the Pardhis do not shave their heads in token of mourning. One *kachcha bhojan* (feast of unfried food) is given on the day of death. On the fifth day *kanya bhoj* (feast to unmarried girls) is given and on the *dashvan* (10th day) and *terhi* (13th day) all relatives are fed.

Depending upon the resources of the family of the deceased and the social status of the latter, a mud, stone or cement concrete platform (*chabutara*), sometimes with a roof over it, is built over the grave. Applique designs of human, animal and bird figures and weapons are made in cement or clay on the inner wall of the tomb. Those who cannot afford to build a *chabutara*, place a few stones on the grave. To propitiate the spirits of the dead, food, flowers, coconuts, incense, etc. are offered on the grave on the eighth day of the months of *kuaanr* (September-October) and *chait* (March-April). If the offering is not made, the soul of the dead turns into an evil spirit and harasses the living.

In the case of the Phanse Pardhis, those who can afford it, cremate their dead, the rest bury them. The corpse is carried to the grave by three men, one holding the head, a second the feet, and a third the waist. On the third day a little molasses and a little clarified butter are laid on the grave. This is the only funeral rite. No other ceremonies are performed to propitiate the deceased ancestors.

Religion

The Pardhis worship the spirits of their ancestors and a number of goddesses. Their principal deities, according to Enthoven, are: *Amba Bhavani*, *Jari Mata* and *Khandoba*. Those residing in the Belgaum District of Karnataka chiefly worship *Lakshmi*, *Durgava* and *Dyamava*; and in Kachchh they worship *Gatrad Mata*. The family goddess of the Chavan clan is the *devi* of the famous Pavagarh hill of Gujarat, while that of the Dabhade, Pawar, Solanki and Sonawani clans being *Chatarshingi* at Saptashring. They also worship all village gods and venerate Muslim saints. When an epidemic breaks out, the gods are propitiated with blood sacrifices. The chief holidays are the Shinga and Dasara. The Pardhis do not go on pilgrimages and have no spiritual head. All their ceremonies, except the funeral, are conducted by Brahmins; funeral ceremonies are conducted by caste elders. According to Russell and Hira Lal (1916), however, in central India the Brahmins do not officiate at their ceremonies. We too did not find any evidence to support Enthoven's statement.

The principal deities of the Phanse Pardhis, according to Enthoven, are Yellamma, Tulja-Bhavani, and Venkatesh, whose images are kept tied in cloth and are taken out once a year on *Ramnavami* in Ashvin, and worshipped with an offering of milk. The Phanse Pardhis do not observe any of the Hindu holidays and make no pilgrimages.

In central India the graves of important ancestors are treated as shrines and images of family deities are installed on the platform over the grave. The spirits of the deceased ancestors as well as the family goddesses are worshipped on sacred days during the year. *Shakti* is the principal deity of the *Jhalawar* clan while *Kalka Devi* is the goddess of the *Solankis*. Other goddesses are *Ishwari Devi*, *Shitala* and *Bhimsen*. A goat is sacrificed to the goddess but no liquor is offered. *Thakur Baba* is a deity worshipped by all Pardhis.

If a child or animal falls sick or a herd or flock is threatened with decimation by an epidemic, the parents of the child or owners of the herd or flock propitiate the family goddess through *puja* (worship), and if the sickness is cured, they give a feast (*bhandara*) to the relatives. On such occasions relatives from many *deras* gather for the feast. For example, during our visit to Umrari village there was a feast in Khaprakhedi-Julanpur village, 45 km west of Umrari. For the *bhandara puris* are prepared in a *kadhai* (deep frying pan). According to Geslal of Umrari village, in his *kuli* the ritual *kadhai* is used only on the occasion of *bhandara*. They can, however, use a normal *kadhai* for preparing dishes for daily consumption.

In Chandarpura village the Pardhis have a shrine in which several silver-plated images of goddesses, some riding a lion, are placed in a row against the back wall of the shrine (Fig. 29). A knife and earthen pots are placed by the side of the images.

Fig. 29. Pardhi shrine at Chandarpura village with images of ancestors

Russell and Hira Lal (1916: 361-62), quoting a Mr. Gayer, state that, "no Langoti Pardhi woman will wear silver below the waist or hang her sari on a peg, as it must never be put on the same level as the goddess. They also sometimes refuse to wear red or coloured clothes, one explanation for this being that the image of the goddess is placed on a red cloth. In Hoshangabad their principal deity is called Guraiya Deo, and his image, consisting of a human figure embossed in silver, is kept in a leather bag on the west side of their tents; and for this reason women going out of the encampment for a necessary purpose always proceed to the east. They also sleep with their feet to the east. Goats are offered to Guraiya Deo and their horns are placed in his leather bag. In Hoshangabad they sacrifice a fowl to the ropes of their tents at the Dasahra and Diwali festivals, and on the former occasion clean their hunting implements and make offerings to them of turmeric and rice."

Because the hunter's calling is largely dependent on luck or chance, the Pardhis believe in various superstitions and omens, and observe various rules by which they think their fortunes will be affected. Russell and Hira Lal (1916: 362) describe many of these as follows:

"A favourite omen is the simple device of taking some rice or *juari* in the hand and counting the grains. Contrary to the usual rule, even numbers are considered lucky and odd ones unlucky. If a winnowing basket or millstone be let fall and drop to the right hand it is a lucky omen, and similarly if a flower from Devi's garland should fall to the right side. The bellowing of cows, the mewing of a cat, the howling of a jackal and sneezing are other unlucky omens. If a snake passes from left to right it is a bad omen and if from right to left a good one. A man must not sleep with his head on the threshold of a house or in the doorway of a tent under penalty of a fine of Rs. 2-8; … A similar penalty is imposed if he falls down before his wife even by accident. A Pardhi, with the exception of members of the Sesodia clan, must never sleep on a cot… A man who has once caught a deer must not again have the hair of his head touched by a razor, and thus the Pardhis may be recognized by their long and unkempt locks. A woman must never step across the rope or peg of a tent, nor upon the place where the blood of a deer has flowed on to the ground. During her monthly period of impurity a woman must not cross a river nor sit in a boat. A Pardhi will never kill or sell a dog and they will not hunt wild dogs even if money is offered to them. This is probably because they look upon the wild dog as a fellow hunter, and consider that to do him injury would bring ill-luck upon themselves."

A Pardhi may not swear by a dog, a cat or a squirrel. Their most solemn oath is in the name of their deity Guraiya Deo, and it is believed that any one who falsely takes this oath will become a leper.

Economy

The Pardhis are extremely poor and possess little by way of property. Their houses are small and modest, being made of stone, mud and thatch. Only a few members of the community have small pieces of cultivable land. Most of them own a bullock to carry their belongings and a few have a cart and a pair of bullocks and some have bicycles. Almost every one owns a few goats and some poultry, a few metal and earthen pots, baskets and other domestic items, and a few pieces of hunting equipment. For example, in Chandarpura hamlet only a few persons like Palangchand and Roslal own land. Bhagirath of Jamunia village has one bullock, seven goats and some poultry. He has a *pada* (a camouflage device) which he hangs near his camp to scare away carnivores that may eat his goats. Vakilchand of the same village has two bullocks, two cows, two calves and a cart; his brother, Kevalchand has a cart, two bullocks and 35 goats. The six sons of Sanwal Singh together own eight acres of land and two bullocks.

The Pardhi economy comprises four principal components, namely (1) hunting, (2) animal husbandry, agriculture and related occupations, (3) trade, and (4) crime. We give below a brief account of each of them.

Hunting

The main occupation of the Pardhi males is hunting, and animal flesh constitutes an essential and important part of their subsistence. They hunt a variety of animals like *suar* or wild boar (*Sus scrofa*), *chitara* or *chital* (*Axis axis*), *sambar* (*Cervus unicolor*), *chausingha* (*Tetracerus quadricornis*), *bhed* or *bhedka* (a deer or antelope), *lukharia* or fox (*Vulpes bengalensis*), *ladajja* or jackal (*Canis aureus*), *rojh* or *nilgai* (*Boselaphus tragocamelus*), *khargosh* or *khara* or hare (*Lepus nigricollis*), porcupine (*Hystrix indica*), and *goh* or monitor lizard (*Varanus bengalensis*). *Bhed* or *bhedka* was described to us by some informants as the female of *chausingha* but some others said it has two antlers and therefore it might be a barking deer or muntjac (*Muntiacus muntjak*). The Pardhis eat *goh* or the ground-dwelling monitor lizard but do not eat *guhera* which lives in tree hollows and is poisonous. They also snare and shoot birds like the *saras* crane (*Grus antigone*), bustard (*Choriotis nigriceps*), *titar* or partridge (*Francolinus pondicerianus*), *bater* or quail (*Streptopelia decaocta*), *mor* or peacock (*Pavo cristatus*), *donkia*, *harel*, *parewa*, and *jalmurgi* (*Phalacrobracs carbosinensis*). Some of them, like the group in the Samnapur forest camp, profess not to hunt and consume *nilgai*, jackal, fox and monitor lizard.

The hunting of large game is now rare partly because such game has become scarce due to rapid deforestation in recent decades, and partly because it is banned by law. However, both in the Chandarpura-Umrari area and around Samnapur, specially in the Mrigannath jungle, animals like *nilgai*, *sambar*, *chausingha* and *chital* are present and are occasionally hunted. In the Samnapur jungle there are also leopards and probably tigers. While we were at Samnapur, a *nilgai* was killed by a leopard. Some villagers of Samnapur brought the left-over part of the carcass and distributed it among themselves for cooking and eating. At Chandarpura, Palangchand had shot a *bhed* a few days before we interviewed him and we were able to collect its lower jaw bone from him. He also offered to shoot a deer for us if we would wait for a few days. Among the medium-sized animals the wild boar is extensively hunted even though this is banned. The reason for the prevalence of this illegal practice is that herds of wild boar cause considerable damage to the crops, and so the farmers encourage the Pardhis to kill these animals. The police also connive at this illegal practice. The hunting of wild boar is done mainly in night when the animals come to feed on the crops. The man who actually kills the boar gets half the meat; other participants in the hunt share the remaining half.

A study of the hunting strategies of three non-pastoral nomadic groups in western Maharashtra by K.C. Malhotra and his colleagues has provided valuable information about the Pardhis (Malhotra *et al.* 1983). The three groups studied were Nandiwallas (who use a trained bull for telling fortune), Vaidus (traditional medicine dispensers) and Phanse Pardhis. The three communities share the same habitat, namely rocky scrub and grassland in a semi-arid environment. But their hunting preferences are clearly distinct and therefore there is minimal conflict among them. The Phanse Pardhis mainly hunt large animals like the blackbuck and wild pig and to a lesser extent snare birds, but the full list includes the following animals and birds: jungle cat, blackbuck, wild pig, monitor lizard, hare, leopard, mongoose, pigeon, dove, partridge, peafowl, *karkunj*, quail and *pakhurdi*. The average biomass of the hunted game per household among the Phanse Pardhis is nearly 3,000 kg per year, the average per capita protein consumption is 101 gm per day and the average per capita calorie intake is 1620 gm per day. These values would be higher but for the fact that the Phanse Pardhis sell a part of the hunted game.

Pardhis are extremely skilled and successful hunters and trappers. The flesh of the animals and birds killed or trapped by them is used for their own consumption as well as sold to villagers for earning cash. They eat the flesh of goat, sheep, deer, fowl, hog, peacock, partridge and quail, and almost all feathered game and fish, as well as drink liquor. In Kachchh, hog, fowl, and feathered game, except for partridge, are prohibited.

In addition to hunting and trapping, the Pardhis also gather wild fruit, tubers, etc. and eat them. Besides, they also collect honey which they sell to people in villages and towns.

Hunting Technology and Techniques

The tools and weapons employed by the Pardhis for hunting and trapping are: the *ballam* or spear, six kinds of traps (namely, 1. *phanda* or *phandi*, 2. *tantla* or *tantli*), 3. *mangri*, 4. *khandara*, 5. *khandaria*, and 6. *kudka*), 7. *phataka* or *phadaka* or explosive balls, and 8. guns. They also use a device called *pada* or *bijuka* and a bullock as a decoy to hide themselves from the birds and animals they intend to attack.

These devices and techniques are briefly described below:

Ballam or spear: This consists of a 20 to 25 cm long triangular iron blade with a socket at one end in which is fixed a bamboo or wooden stick about 1.5 m long. The weapon is used for killing the animal while held in the hand or by throwing it at a fleeing animal. It is used for hunting wild boar, deer and other relatively large animals.

Lathi: This is a 2 m long bamboo stick which can be effectively used for killing wild boar when the animal is cornered, as also for killing hare.

Guns: Prosperous Pardhis have guns which they use for shooting wild boar and deer.

Phanda or *Phandi* or *Tantla* (Fig. 30) is a very large (over 10 m long) snare which is formed of multiple nooses made of animal sinew. The nooses are tied to small (about 20-25 cm long) wooden sticks which are vertically fixed in the ground in a straight line. The nooses stand above the sticks. The trap is laid in a place frequented by wild boar, deer and other animals. The moment an animal steps on one of the nooses, it closes and traps the foot of the animal. When the animal tries to run, it gets snared in more nooses and it is easy for the hunter to injure or kill it with a spear. When not in use, the *tantla* is kept in a circular basket of goat skin at the bottom of which several vulture skins are placed to provide cushioning and prevent damage to the equipment. The basket is covered by a goatskin lid. The white skins of vultures are spread in front of the mouth of *tantla*. The birds run towards the skins attracted by them.

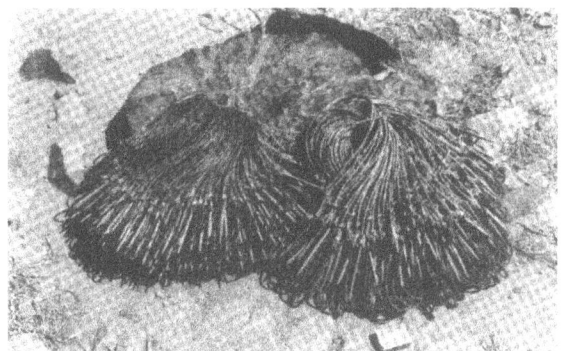

Fig. 30. *Phanda / Phandi / Tantla*, snare used by the Pardhis

Tantli: Made of much smaller nooses, this is a smaller version of the *tantla*, and is used for snaring hares and birds.

Mangri: (Fig. 31). A cylindrical trap, this is about 2.5 m long and is woven from cotton or nylon string. It is about 50 cm wide at the mouth and tapers toward the tip. The trap is placed on the ground, its mouth is kept open by means of a vertical stick, and grains are scattered inside it. The hunter sits at a distance holding the string, one end of which is tied to the end of the trap. When the birds enter the trap to eat the grain, the hunter closes the mouth of the trap by pulling the string and thereby prevents the birds from escaping.

Fig. 31. *Mangri*, a cylindrical trap used by the Pardhis for trapping birds

Khandara: (Fig. 32). This is a trap made of bamboo sticks and nylon string. The bamboo sticks are tied together to form small square compartments to which nooses made of nylon string are tied. The trap can be folded into a compact rectangular shape when not in use. It is spread out in a place frequented by birds and grains are scattered in front of it. When the birds come to eat the grain, they unwittingly put their head or foot on the noose which because of the weight of the bird's body tightens around its neck or foot. It is used mainly for trapping partridge. The trapper fixes the *khandara* where he notices *bater* or *titar*, then moves towards them under the camouflage of *pada* and when the birds are near the trap, he pushes them into the *khandara*.

Fig. 32. *Khandara*, a trap used by the Pardhis for trapping birds

Khandaria: A smaller version of the *khandara*, it is used for trapping small birds like quail and *donkia*.

Kudka: This is an iron trap consisting of two large loops. It is fixed on the ground with the two loops stretched sideways and lightly suspended on hooks. When an animal steps on the trap, the loops are released and trap the animal's foot in a vice-like grip. The *kudka* is used for trapping wild boar, deer, jackal, fox and hare. It is identical to the *kudka* used by the Van Vagris (Fig. 15).

Phadaka or Phataka or Explosives: These are small table tennis-sized balls made by placing explosive powder inside flour. They are prepared by Muslims who are in the business of manufacturing fireworks and Pardhis buy the balls from them. Several such balls are placed in the openings of fences of fields frequented by wild boar and other animals. The balls are sprinkled with kerosene and covered with green leaves. The animal, attracted by the smell of kerosene, comes to eat the leaves and unsuspectingly takes the explosive ball in its mouth. When the animal tries to crush the ball with its jaws, it explodes, killing or seriously wounding it. This technique is mainly employed for killing wild boar.

The use of the explosive balls is dangerous and sometimes leads to accidents. Pittal Singh of Chandarpura died in a blast caused by explosive balls. There were some fifty balls tied together and he was cutting the string when the explosion occurred. He was seriously injured and died on the way to hospital. Before dying, however, he made a declaration to the police that he was injured by an army grenade which he picked up in the forest, not knowing that it could explode. Several other persons sitting nearby were also injured in the blast. In yet another incident, about three years ago, Nap Singh and Gulab Singh, along with some other Pardhis of Chandarpura village, were hunting jackals with explosives in the neighbourhood of Kareli. By accident a farmer's dog was killed. The farmer lodged a complaint with the police and as result all the Pardhis in the area were arrested. The explosive was, however, found only with these two brothers. They were prosecuted but released on bail after one year. The case was still going on in the court several years after the incident took place.

Except for the iron *kudka* which is made by ironsmiths and guns which they buy from the market, all other equipment is made by the Pardhis themselves. They are extremely skillful in making complex items using string and sticks, particularly horse-hair nooses. They also sell the hunting equipment made by them to other hunting-gathering communities like the Kuchbandhias. Several Pardhis at Chandarpura had guns besides other equipment, and the group in the Samnapur forest camp had dogs, *ballam*, *lathi*, explosive balls and several kinds of traps and snares.

The Pardhis also use trained dogs for hunting wild boar, deer and hare though every hunter does not own such dogs. For example, Pojam and his brothers at Chandarpura did not own any dogs. In addition, they use a bull, specially trained for the purpose, as a decoy in hunting and trapping (Fig. 33). The hunter gently guides the bull towards the prey (deer or birds), hiding himself by its side. When the bull is close to the birds, it shakes its head on prompting by the hunter. The birds get scared and run towards the net and are trapped. The man then quickly closes the mouth of the net. As the animals and birds are accustomed to the presence of bulls and other animals, they are taken by surprise when the hunter attacks them from close range. The Pardhis also use a device called a *pada* or *bijuka* (Fig. 34) in hunting. It is made of a rectangular piece of cloth fixed on a rectangular bamboo frame. The cloth is painted brown and stippled in orange. The hunter hides himself behind the *pada* but is able to see the objects in front of him through two narrow slits in the cloth. He walks stealthily toward the unsuspecting prey and attacks it at close range.

Fig. 33. A Pardhi riding a bull which is used as a decoy for hunting animals and birds

Fig. 34. *Pada / Bijuka* used by the Pardhis as a camouflage device for hunting

Russell and Hira Lal (1916: 365-66) have quoted a description of the hunting techniques of the Phanse Pardhis as given by V. Ball in his book, *Jungle Life in India*:

"For peacock, *saras* crane and bustard they have a long series of nooses, each provided with a wooden peg and all connected with a long string. The tension necessary to keep the nooses open is afforded by a slender slip of antelope's horn (very much resembling whalebone), which forms the core of the loop. Provided with several sets of these nooses, a trained bullock and shield-like cloth screen dyed buff and pierced with eye-holes, the bird-catcher sets out for the jungle, and on seeing a flock of pea-fowl circles round them under cover of the screen and the bullock, which he guides by a nose-string. The birds feed on undisturbed, and the man rapidly pegs out his long strings of nooses, and when all are properly disposed, moves round to the opposite side of the birds and shows himself; when they of course run off, and one or more getting their feet in the nooses fall forwards and flap on the ground; the man immediately captures them, knowing that if the strain is relaxed the nooses will open and permit the bird's escape. Very cruel practices are in vogue with these people with reference to the captured birds, in order to keep them alive until a purchaser is found. The peacocks have a feather passed through the eyelids, by which means they are effectively blinded, while in the case of smaller birds both the legs and wings are broken".

"Deer, hares and even pig are also caught by a strong rope with running nooses. For smaller birds the appliance is a little rack about four inches high with uprights a few inches apart, between each of which is hung a noose. Another appliance mentioned by Mr. Ball is a set of long conical bag nets, which are kept open by hooks and provided with a pair of folding doors. The Pardhi has also a whistle made of deer-horn, with which he can imitate the call of the birds. Tree birds are caught with bird-lime as described by Sir G. Grierson (*Peasant Life in Bihar*, p. 80). The Bahelia has several long shafts of bamboos called *nal* or *nar*, which are tied together like a fishing rod, the endmost one being covered with bird-lime. Concealing himself behind his bamboo screen the Bahelia approaches the bird and when near enough strikes and secures it with his rod; or he may spread some grain out at a short distance, and as the birds are hopping about over it he introduces the pole, giving it a zig-zag movement and imitating as far as possible the progress of a snake. Having brought the point near one of the birds, which is fascinated by its stealthy approach, he suddenly jerks it into its breast and then drawing it to him, releases the poor palpitating creature, putting it away in his bag, and recommences the same operation. This method does not require the use of bird-lime."

Almost certainly the equipment described by Ball refers to the *phanda, tantli, pada, khandara, khandaria* and *mangri* described, demonstrated and sold to us by our Pardhi informants.

The technique employed by the Chita Pardhis using the cheetah (*Felis jubata*) to catch deer has been described by Russell and Hira Lal (1916: 366-67) after the account given of it by Jerdon in his book, *Mammals of India*, p.97, and quoted in the Chhindwara District Gazetteer (pp. 16-17):

"The leopard is caught full-grown by a noose in the manner related above. Its neck is first clasped in a wooden vice until it is half-strangled, and its feet are then bound with ropes and a cap slipped over its head. It is partially starved for a time, and being always fed by the same man, after a month or so it becomes tame and learns to know its master. It is then led through villages held by ropes on each side to accustom it to the presence of human beings. On a hunting party the leopard is carried on a cart, hooded, and, being approached from down wind, the deer allow the cart to get fairly close to them. The Indian antelope or the blackbuck are the usual quarry, and as these frequent the cultivated land, they regard country carts without suspicion. The hood is then taken off and the leopard springs forward at the game with extreme velocity, perhaps exceeding that which any other quadruped possesses. The accounts given by Jerdon say that for the moment its speed is greater than that of a race-horse. It cannot maintain this for more than three or four hundred yards, and, if in that distance the animal has not seized its prey, it relinquishes the pursuit and stalks about in a towering passion. The Pardhis say that when it misses the game the leopard is as sulky as a human being and sometimes refuses food for a couple of days. If successful in the pursuit, it seizes the antelope by the throat; the keeper then comes up, and cutting the animal's throat collects some of the blood in the wooden ladle with which the leopard is always fed; this is offered to him, and dropping his hold he laps it up eagerly, when the hood is cleverly slipped on again."

"The conducting of the cheetah from its cage to the chase is by no means an easy matter. The keeper leads him along, as he would a large dog, with a chain; and for a time as they scamper over the country the leopard goes willingly enough; but if anything arrest his attention, some noise from the forest, some scented trail upon the ground, he moves more slowly, throws his head aloft and peers savagely round. A few more minutes perhaps and he would be unmanageable. The keeper, however, is prepared for the emergency. He holds in his left hand a coconut shell, sprinkled on the inside with salt; and by means of a handle affixed to the shell he puts it at once over the nose of the cheetah. The animal licks the salt, loses the scent, forgets the object which arrested his attention, and is led quietly along again. (*Private Life of an Eastern King*, p. 75)."

"For catching crocodile, a method by which one group of the Pardhis earn their livelihood, a large double hook is used, baited with a piece of putrid deer's flesh and attached to a hempen rope 70 or 80 feet long. When the crocodile has swallowed the hook, twenty or thirty persons drag the animal out of water and it is despatched with axes. Crocodiles are hunted only in the month of Pus (December), Magh (January) and Chait (March), when they are generally fat and yield plenty of oil. The flesh is cut into pieces and stewed over a slow fire, when it exudes a watery oil. This is strained and sold in bottles at a rupee a seer (2 lbs). It is used as an embrocation for rheumatism and for neck galls of cattle. The Pardhis do not eat crocodile's flesh."

Even though the Pardhis live primarily by hunting and trapping, they are conscious of the importance of conserving wildlife. When a Pardhi has caught a number of birds in his trap, he will let a pair of them loose so that they may go on breeding (Russell and Hira Lal 1916: 363).

Trade

Having been obliged for centuries to live in close proximity to villages and towns and in an environment which has been steadily depleted of wild plants and animals, the Pardhis had to look for other resources, besides hunting and gathering, to earn cash to meet their requirements of utensils, clothing, jewellery and expenditure on social and religious events like birth, marriage, death and festivals. They have always procured food grains and other items by bartering a part of the hunted meat, animal skins and honey. A *titar* is sold for Rs. 10 and a *bater* for Rs. 2.50. There is a good market for meat because except for Brahmins, Banias and some Rajputs, all the castes eat it. Some of the Pardhis also make and sell baskets to farmers and hunting gear to other hunting-gathering communities.

The major component of their economy, however, is petty trade which is practised almost exclusively by their women (Fig. 27). The trading occupation is known as *manihari*, and it consists of selling of *chudis* (bangles), cosmetics and trinkets to village women. The Pardhis buy these goods wholesale from the town markets. Earlier they sold only cheap jewellery and cosmetics but in recent years they have started selling bangles as well. They say that initially they did not know how to slip bangles onto the wrist but they learnt it by practice. Although both men and women practise this trade, by its very nature it is primarily a female occupation. The women go to villages carrying their goods in baskets on their heads. They travel for 30-40 km by bus and foot and return after 3-4 days. When they are in a camp, the women go out for *manihari* trade and the men stay in the camp to look after the children and goats. Some men go off to sell perfumes and medicines. The cash earnings of Pardhi families come largely from this source.

Unlike the Kuchbandhias with whom they share their environment, the Pardhis do not make and sell articles of rope nor crockery. They have probably taken to *manihari* trade to carve out an independent economic niche for themselves, and avoid competition and conflict with the Kuchbandhias. According to Enthoven

(1922), a division of the Pardhis, called Jogires in Dharwar, make blackstone vessels of various sizes which are used for storing pickles and sometimes for cooking.

Pittal Singh and some others of Chandarpura used to catch and sell monkeys for medical research but now as there is a ban on the export of monkeys, this occupation is finished.

Animal Husbandry, Agriculture and Other Occupations

Almost every Pardhi owns some livestock, mainly goats and fowl and occasionally bullocks. The goats not only supply milk and meat but are also sold to earn cash. They are also kept for offering as sacrifice to the mother goddess. Some Pardhis also have small plots of land which they cultivate and increasingly more and more of them are taking to this occupation.

Some Pardhis, like the Van Vagris in Rajasthan, seek employment for protecting the crops of local farmers from wild animals and domestic livestock and for this they are paid in the form of grain at the end of the harvest. Those who have no land of their own cultivate the land of other farmers as share croppers or simply work as manual labourers in the fields. For example, Vakilchand of Jamunia village stopped hunting about five years ago and as he does not own any land, he cultivates others' land. Similarly, Shivram and Jumman, both landless, work as labourers, mainly doing harvesting of crops for which they are paid in grain. Some work as village watchmen and servants, and some, specially old women, beg. A section of the community, known as Takankars and found mainly in Vidarbha, travel about roughening the stones of the household grinding mills when their surfaces have worn smooth. For this they receive an annual contribution of grain from each household. In Kachchh the Pardhis are known to be snake charmers and catch snakes. Geslal's father was a good flute player and mimicry specialist.

Like the Kuchbandhias, the Pardhis also perform certain pseudo-religious functions. For example, some of them claim to have powers to prevent the occurrence of natural calamities like rain and hail which would damage the farmers' crops. Through the incantation of some magical formulae and by performing some rituals they seal, so to say, the borders of a given area (*medo bandhna*) against rain and hail. When we went to Aanvaria village, Bhagirath's maternal uncle had gone out for this purpose. They also know medicinal plants, roots, etc. and dispense medicines. They claim to heal bone fractures by applying the powder of a root called *Hadjudi* on the limb which has suffered injury.

Crime

Like most of the other hunting-gathering communities sharing their habitat with villagers and towns people, Pardhis too are given to crime. According to Enthoven, though they had taken to comparatively peaceful habits, they had not got rid of their thieving propensities. When in towns and villages for selling game, they try to find a suitable place for robbery. They commit burglaries, rob fields, and steal when the chance offers. About the Phanse Pardhis, Enthoven (1922: 173) says:

"Though ostensibly snarers and hunters, they make their living mainly by committing robberies. They openly rob the standing crops. The landlords stand in such awe of them that they secure their goodwill by submitting to a regular system of blackmail. If they refuse to let the ears be taken, they would run a good chance of losing the whole crop when it was gathered in the threshing floor."

Russell and Hira Lal (1916: 369-70), quoting a Mr. Sewell, state that the "Langoti Pardhis and Takankars are the worst offenders. Ordinarily when committing dacoity they are armed with sticks and stones only. In digging through a wall they generally leave a thin strip at which the leader carefully listens before finally bursting through. Then when the hole has been made large enough, he strikes a match and holding it in front of him so that his features are shielded has a good survey of the room before entering…. As a rule, they do not divide the property on or near the scene of crime, but take it home. Generally it is carried by one of the gang well behind the rest so as to enable it to be hidden if the party is challenged. In Bombay they openly rob the standing crops, and the landlords are such awe of them that they secure their goodwill by submitting to a regular system of blackmail."

Because of their propensity for crime, all members of the community are treated by the police as criminals. Whenever there is a case of theft or robbery, the tendency of the police is to round up the Pardhis of the neighbourhood for questioning. In Sagar district when a group of Pardhis go out for a social function, they have to first report their presence at the local police station. Like the other hunting-gathering communities given to crime, the Pardhis too probably took to crime as their forest habitat was destroyed and their hunting-gathering way of life became unviable.

Panchayat

The *Panchayat* plays a very important role in the life of the Pardhis. It consists of selected elders of the clan. The Pardhis avoid going to the police and courts to resolve their disputes. All disputes are referred to the *Panchayat* and the verdict given by it is binding on both the disputing parties. During our field work we were witness to the functioning of the *Panchayat* in a dispute which involved a woman who had deserted her husband and started living with another man. Since the dispute involved two different clans, each party had nominated a fixed number of *panches* (members of the (*panchayat*) who would informally elect one member from amongst themselves as the chief *panch*. The *panches* held many sittings, but did not reach a verdict. The sittings were always held away from the village in the open where no outsiders will have access to the ongoing proceedings, We were, however, permitted to sit and watch the proceedings because we were introduced to an influential member of the *Panchayat* through one of our informants who knew him. The *panches* would ask questions to the disputants and would demand proof to support their statements. The disputants as well as the witnesses had to swear in the name of their goddess to convince the *panches* that they were telling the truth. After hearing them the *panches* would decide the place, date and time of the next sitting and would adjourn the meeting. It was very obvious to outsiders like us that they were deliberately adopting delaying tactics in reaching a verdict because during each sitting they were being offered unlimited liquor and good food by the disputants. Perhaps the disputants were aware of this strategy but they had no choice except to wait until the *panches* had reached a decision.

Economic and Social Change

During the British period, the Pardhis, like many other hunting-gathering communities, were classified as a Criminal

Tribe. This pejorative designation was, however, withdrawn after Independence. Today even though many of them continue to engage in hunting and gathering as a partial source of subsistence and live a nomadic way of life, some of them are taking to other occupations and becoming partially settled or semi-nomadic. As a part of its policy for improving the economic and social status of the weaker sections of society, the government is now providing them with housing and agricultural plots, as well as loans for the purchase of agricultural equipment, bullocks and goats, and for building houses. For example, Rameshwar and Kevalchand of Jamunia village have been given four and three acres of land, respectively by the government. However, the land given to the Pardhis by the government is usually rocky and stony, and therefore largely unfit for agriculture. Some are able to purchase land on their own. For example, Satal, son of Jujhar Singh, had purchased eight acres. His sons sold 1.5 acres to meet the expenses of the funeral ceremonies of their father.

Some Pardhis have taken to business or have got government jobs after acquiring some education. For example, Shivram's maternal uncle, Chandu Seth (now deceased), was a vegetable dealer in Nasik, Maharashtra. According to Shivram he had a truck, a jeep and a motor cycle. He has two sons one of whom is a businessman and lives near Nasik railway station and the other is a Police officer. The prosperous Pardhis now live in pucca houses. However, by and large, most Pardhis continue to remain extremely poor. Their nomadic lifestyle prevents their children from going to school and from taking advantage of the reservations provided to them in government jobs. It will take a few generations for them to be completely assimilated into the mainstream society.

3. The Kuchbandhias

The Kuchbandhias are another hunting-gathering community found in central India. The name Kuchbandhia is derived from the Hindi word `kuch' meaning brush. In earlier days one of the main occupations of the community was making brushes for use by the village weavers for cleaning yarn. However, this occupation was slowly given up as factory-made cloth became cheaper and more popular and the handloom weaving industry declined. W. Crooke and several other ethnographers are of the opinion that the Kuchbandhias are only a section of the bigger Kanjar tribe but the Kuchbandhias themselves stoutly deny any relationship with the Kanjars. The Kuchbandhias share the same habitat as the Pardhis, and their cultures are also fairly similar. Like the Pardhis the Kuchbandhias also have a permanent base either in a regular multi-caste village or in an independent hamlet outside the main village, but most of the poor members of the community are on the move except during the rainy season.

Much of the information on the community was provided to us by Bijai Singh (Fig. 35), son of Gulab Singh, a Kuchbandhia from Sajli village, located by the side of Sagar-Jabalpur road in Sagar district, about one km from Parsonia bus stand and the same distance from Girbar railway station. There are four Kuchbandhia families in this village. They came here about 35 years ago from Bamori *Tigadda* (tri-junction) near Sagar town. Although Bijai Singh has a permanent house in Sajli village where one of his wives and most of the children live, he. along with one of the wives, Draupadi and a few children moves around most of the time. While he does hunting, his wife sells crockery in the villages. We first met Bijai Singh and his wife while they were camping under a tree outside Samnapur village. Afterwards he was regularly coming to our excavation camp and providing us information about his community. Bijai Singh's nephews, who live in Makronia, a subsurb of Sagar town, also wander around hunting and come to live in Makronia only during the rainy season.

Fig. 35. Kuchbandhias on way to hunting expedition at Sajli village

In Killai village, three km south of Damoh town in Damoh district, there are about 50 Kuchbandhia families. There is a large population of the community, numbering about 500 individuals in Kareli town of Sagar district. A few families of the community are found in most of the villages in Sagar and Damoh districts.

3.1 Social Organisation

According to Bijai Singh, following *gots* or clans are found among the Kuchbandhias: Bhains, Untwar, Purbia, Rara, Soda, Sankas, Mewati, Luhiya, Khandeshia (those who came from Khandesh in Maharashtra) and Guhera. Although some of these names are also found among the Kanjars, Bijai Singh disclaims any connection of his community with the Kanjars. Polygamy is common in the community. Bijay Singh, at the age of 46 had three wives and 22 children. Divorce and remarriage are permitted for both men and women. To overcome the problem of bride price exchange marriage, whereby two persons marry each other's sister, is often resorted to.

3.2 Religion

The principal deity of the Kuchbandhias is *Bhainsasur* or Buffalo god. Their goddesses are *Nav Durga*, *Marai Devi* (goddess of small pox), *Hinglaj Devi* and *Khisi Devi*, the last one being the most revered. The deities are represented by a silver image, and the entire family has one common image for worship.

3.3 Hunting

The chief occupation of Kuchbandhia men is hunting. In olden days, when game was plentiful, they used to hunt the following animals: 1. Sambar (*Cervus unicolor*), 2. Chital (*Axis axis*), 3. Rojh (*Boselaphus tragocamelus*), 4. Wild boar (*Sus scrofa*), 5. Bhed (a kind of deer or antelope), 6. Khara or hare (*Lepus nigricollis*), 7. Salua or Pangolin (*Manis crassicaudata* Gray), 8. Sehi or porcupine (*Hystrix indica*) 9. *Mirga* (*Antilope cervicapra*), 10. *Lukharia* or fox (*Vulpes bengalensis*), 11. *Ladajja* or jackal (*Canis aureus*), 12. *Nevra* or mongoose (*Herpestes edwardsi*), 13. *Goi* or *Goera* or monitor lizard (*Varanus bengalensis*). The informants mentioned several other animals like *Puskara*, *Maua Chonkha* and *Musak* but from the description provided by them it is not possible to correctly identify them. Among the birds trapped by them, partridge (*Francolinus pondicerianus*) and *bater* or quail (*Streptopelia decaocta*) are the most common. However, these days only small game is hunted because large game has become scarce and its hunting is prohibited by the government.

The technology and techniques used by the Kuchbandhias are similar to those used by the Pardhis. However, we did not hear from any informant about the use of the *pada* (camouflage device) and of bull as a decoy by the Kuchbandhias. The Kuchbandhias buy their hunting gear usually from the Pardhis. They are particularly adept in hunting wild boar. For this, like the Pardhis, they use explosive powder kept inside a ball made of flour. They place several balls in an opening in the fence of a field and sprinkle kerosene over it. When the boar, attracted by the scent of kerosene, takes the ball in its mouth, it explodes, killing or severely injuring the animal. Bijai Singh demonstrated to us the use of the explosive balls by placing them in the fence along the edge of a field. The hunting of the wild boar is welcomed by the farmers as the animal is a menace to their crops.

3.4. Other Occupations

Many Kuchbandhia men, particularly in Kareli town, are engaged in the illicit manufacture and selling of liquor made of *Mahua* (*Madhuca indica*) flowers. The Inspector at the Kareli Police station told us that he overlooks this activity because if the Kuchbandhia are deprived of this source of income, they would engage in more serious crimes to earn their livelihood and will become a bigger nuisance to his department. He also told us that the Kuchbandhias take contracts of both country and foreign liquor shops for which they have to pay between 25,000 and 50,000 rupees. They also deal in other narcotics like *bhang* and *ganja*. One of the main occupations of the Kuchbandhias is buying pig hair from pig owners and selling it to factories which make brushes and other articles from the hair. The Kuchbandhia women sell porcelain cups and saucers and porcelain and glass containers to village women. As the wares traded by them are totally different from those of the Pardhis, there is no conflict between the two communities.

3.5. Change

A number of Kuchbandhias have got education and are employed in schools as teachers and in various capacities in other government departments. In Kareli town we visited several Kuchbandhia families whose members have acquired school and college education, have government jobs, and are living a decent life like members of the non-tribal communities. However, it is only those members of the community who have settled down that are able to take advantage of the opportunities for education and employment. The government should make more effort to settle all the nomadic members of the community and encourage them to send their children to schools.

4. The Bawarias

The Bawarias are another community in the area which lives mainly by crime. They derive their name from *Bawar* or noose which was the main device used by them for hunting. Bawaria gangs travel long distances to commit crimes. Some years ago a gang was involved in stealing gold jewellery worth several hundred thousand rupees from a temple at Jabalpur. The court case about this theft, which dragged on for several years, received wide publicity in the press, and the police department even brought out a booklet on it. As recently as 13 June 2007 the TV channel *Aaj Tak* reported that several Bawarias were arrested by the police in the Sarojini Nagar locality of Lucknow in Uttar Pradesh.

SIGNIFICANCE OF HUNTER-FORAGER LIFEWAYS FOR INTERPRETATION OF ARCHAEOLOGICAL DATA

The hunter-forager communities we have described from the Ganga Plains, Rajasthan and Central India live in very contrasting environments and have adapted themselves to those environments in their own distinctive ways. We may briefly recapitulate what we have stated about the communities in the preceding chapters and point out the significance of their lifeways for understanding archaeological data.

6.1 Ganga Plains

The communities of the Ganga plains comprise Aheriya, Badhik, Baheliya, Bandi, Bangali, Bawaria, Bhantu, Gandhila, Gidiya, Habura, Kanjar, Sansi and Siyarmar. Most of these names are derived from Sanskrit or Hindi words and have obviously been given by other people. The meanings of the names are expressive of the economic status and lifestyle of these peoples. Thus Aheriya is thought to be derived from 'Akhetaka' meaning 'hunter', Badhik from '*Vadhaka*' meaning a killer, Baheliya from '*Vyadha*' meaning 'one who pierces, wounds' or kills; Kanjar from '*Kanan Char*', meaning 'wanderer in the jungle', Gandhila from '*Gandh*', meaning 'fetid' or 'malodorous'; and Bawaria or Baori from *Bawar* meaning noose which they use for hunting.

The communities of the Ganga plains live on a flat, extremely fertile alluvial plain which receives ample rainfall and has adequate availability of water from numerous perennial and seasonal rivers, lakes and ponds. Until the middle of the twentieth century there were large tracts of forest even in the upper and middle parts of the plain which receives much less rain than the lower part. Ethnographic accounts of the later part of the nineteenth century show that the ancestors of these communities were living in a forested environment. Some of the groups of Kanjars are said to be never leaving the forest, and some of them used to give a patch of the forest as dowry to their son-in-law where he had exclusive right to hunt and collect forest produce. Some groups disposed of their dead by leaving the corpse in the forest. They were collecting a wide variety of forest produce like honey, gum, wax, *khaskhas* grass and medicinal herbs. Wildlife was plentiful even outside the forest tracts. Large herds of blackbuck and *nilgai* could be seen in the vicinity of villages. Hyenas, wolves, foxes, jackals, monitor lizards, jungle cats, and a large variety of birds were plentiful. The hunter-gatherers had established a symbiotic relationship with Hindu as well as Muslim communities living in the villages and towns. Kanjars, for example, would come and collect honey from beehives in the thatched roofs of the villagers' houses as well as from the trees in their orchards. They also used to hunt small game from fields having standing crops of sugarcane, pigeon pea, *jowar*, *bajra*, etc. Besides, they used to collect turtles from rivers and ponds and turtle eggs from their banks. Beria women used to dance at the functions of lower caste people. Habura men used to go around begging in such a loud and raucous voice that it would frighten the children. . .

All the hunter-gatherers were originally living a nomadic life in small bands of rarely more than five families. The family was invariably nuclear. However, on special occasions like, birth, marriage, death, *puja* of the clan goddess during

Navratra of *Ashvin* (September-October) and *Chaitra* (March-April) a number of bands come together. Each family made its separate hut for keepings its meagre belongings and for small children to sleep. As all families were engaged in hunting, more refuse in the form of charred and broken animal bones was created around the hearth and in the surroundings of the residential area than would be the case if the families of individual bands alone were staying at the same place.

All the three regions have a long history of human occupation. In the Ganga plains the oldest occupation may probably go back to the Late Middle Palaeolithic period. It occurs at the site of Kalpi in Orai district of U.P. in the alluvial deposit of the Yamuna river. The occupation consists of unifacial as well bifacial tools on small quartz pebbles and a variety of forms on charred bones which may be called scrapers. The stone and bone tools are associated with a very rich fossil fauna.

Much richer evidence of human occupation comes from the plain north of the Ganga river comprising Allahabad, Pratapgarh, Sultanpur, Jaunpur and Varanasi districts. Here during the seventies of the last century the late G.R. Sharma and his colleagues at the Department of Ancient History, Culture and Archaeology, of Allahabad University discovered a few epipalaeolithic and over 200 Mesolithic sites. Most of these sites are located along lakes formed by cut-off meanders of streams (Fig. 36). Many of them cover an area of only a few square metres and contain only a small quantity of quartz and chert artefacts comprising flakes, microblades, fluted and simple cores, side and end scrapers, and bits of animal and sometimes even human bones. These may be called sites of category A. There are other sites, much smaller in number, which cover an area of several hundred square metres or over an acre and contain large quantities of stone artefacts comprising debitage as well as microliths, various types of scrapers and points, charred and broken animal bones in large quantities, and human burials containing one or more skeletons. Floors made of burnt clay clods and containing hearths with charred animal bones, charcoal, and ash are also found at these sites, which may be called sites of category B. Three of the category B sites, namely, Sarai-Nahar-Rai, Mahadaha and Damdama have been horizontally excavated. They have yielded large cemeteries with 15 to 40 burials, rich microlithic industry, grinding stones, structural remains, bone and antler tools and ornaments, and plentiful animal remains. (Sharma 1973; Sharma *et al.* 1980; Pal 1984, 1987; Varma *et al.* 1985; Kennedy 2000; Kennedy *et al.* 1986; V.D. Misra 2007). Category A sites may be interpreted to represent short term or transitory occupations by a few individuals comprising one or two families whereas category B sites may be interpreted as representing sedentary or semi-sedentary settlements of the stage when several hunter-gatherer bands, probably belonging to more than one clan settled down at one place.

The Vindhyan plateau south of the Ganga has yielded many Neolithic sites. A few of these like Koldihwa, Mahagara, Tokwa (Misra *et al.*), Tila and Senuwar have been excavated. They have yielded small round-based ground celts of the northeast Indian tradition, osteological remains of both domesticated and wild fauna, remains of both wild and domesticated rice, and cord-marked pottery. Radiocarbon dates give the age of these sites between 2000 and 5000 B.C.

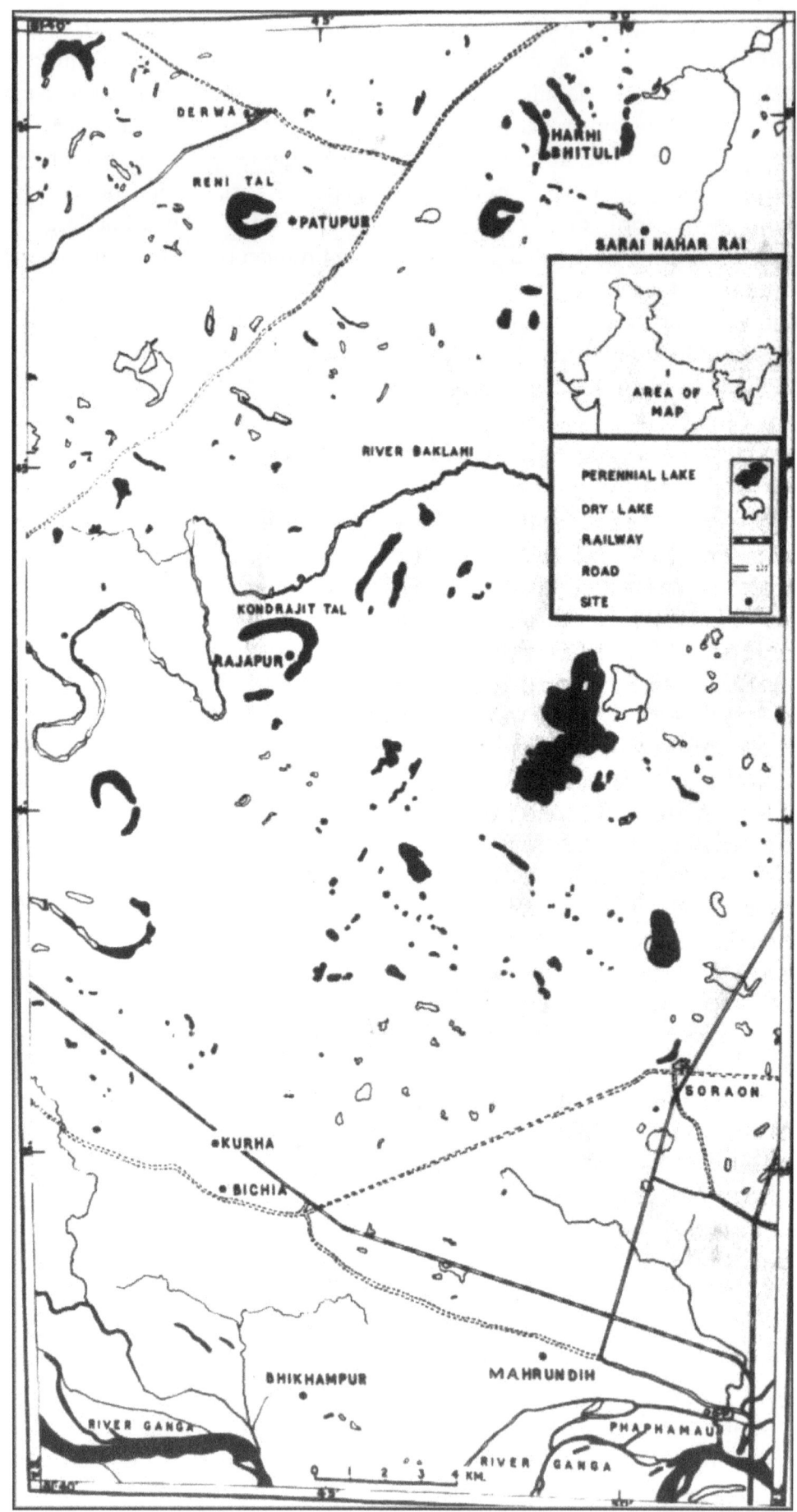

Fig. 36. Mesolithic sites on the shores of lakes in Allahabad and Pratapgarh districts, U.P.

Both north and south of the Ganga a number of Chalcolithic sites have been located and several of these have been excavated, particularly in the Saryupar region, that is, north of the Ghaghra river. These include Jhusi, Hetapatti, Sohgaura, Narhan, Agiabir, Imlidih, Khairadih, and Lahuradeva. They have yielded wattle-and-daub structures, sturdy painted Black-and-Red, Black-on-Red, and Grey Ware ceramics, copper tools, and terracotta beads and animal figurines.

Shahida Ansari (2005) has carried out a detailed ethnographic study of the simple communities, namely Kols, Musahars, and Mallahs living in Allahabad district and looked for similarities between their lifeways and those of the people of the Mesolithic, Neolithic and Chalcolithic cultures. The Kols and Musahars live primarily by hunting small game like hare, jackal, fox, porcupine and monitor lizard. The Musahars are particularly fond of catching and eating rats and squirrels. Both communities also make plates and cups of *palas* leaves and sell them to sweetmeat sellers and traders. The latter sell them to village and town people for use during feasts. The Mallahs are boatmen and fishermen but they also practise horticulture growing fruits like watermelon, muskmelon, and cucumber and vegetables like white gourd and pumpkin in the sandy bed of the Ganga and other streams. All the three communities have their permanent homes in their exclusive hamlets or in multi-caste villages away from the river, and they have their temporary settlements on the river bed or near the edge of the river. The Mallahs also have their temporary settlements on hill tops or rock outcrops from where they can keep a watch on their horticulture plots. Both Kols and Mallahs also practise some regular plough agriculture growing both summer and winter crops while the Musahars only engage in hunting small animals, making leaf cups and plates, and working as labourers.

Ansari noted that except during the rains cooking is done in the open courtyard of the houses on U-shaped *chulhas* as well as on makeshift ovens made of a few stones or brickbats. Foxes, jackals, rats, squirrels and other small creatures hunted by the Kols and Musahars are roasted on open fires while cooking of regular dishes like curry, *dal*, rice and *roti* is done on *chulhas*. Ansari also carried out a study of the refuse disposal and found that it is discarded not far from the houses. All the three communities bury their dead not far from their permanent settlements.

Ansari finds that the way of life of these hunter-gatherer communities practising limited agriculture is considerably similar to that of the Mesolithic hunter-gatherers who too had temporary as well as permanent settlements. The majority of the Mesolithic sites yield only a few microliths and bone fragments over an area of a few square metres, and these probably represent short term or transitory camps of a few families. On the other hand, the three excavated sites, each spread over an acre or more and possessing large cemeteries, represent sedentary or semi-sedentary occupations.

In our view the living hunting-foraging communities of the Ganga plains are almost certainly descendants of the Mesolithic hunter-gatherers, and they can be assumed to be continuing some of the traditions of their prehistoric forbears in their settlement and subsistence patterns, technology and material culture. The way of life of these living hunter-foragers can therefore provide valuable clues for interpreting archaeological data from

Mesolithic sites. For example, in the nineteenth century the Kanjars were known to be living a largely nomadic, life camping in the forest tracts and subsisting on wild animals and plants. Several bands, however, will come together during the rainy season for ceremonial and social activities. It is likely that the small and culturally poor Mesolithic sites represent normal mobile camps of the Kanjars and other hunting-foraging communities while the bigger sites with large cemeteries represent the sedentary or semi-sedentary camps of such communities. The large variety of wild animals exploited by these hunting-foraging communities for food may be representative of Mesolithic exploitative patterns. The hunting tools and techniques of the communities may again give us some idea of the techniques employed by the prehistoric people. The crafts of the hunter-foragers based on making of ropes and rope articles, baskets, reed objects like *sarki* (tents) and grass objects like *idundi* and hide processing may reflect similar craft skills among the Mesolithic people.

6.2 Rajasthan

The northeastern and western part of Rajasthan is an extension of the Indo-Gangetic plain but it gets progressively drier towards the west. The communities which practise hunting-gathering today or were doing so until recently include Bhils, Bagris, Bawarias, Aheriyas, Sansis and Kal Beliyas. Bhils are found all over the State except the northern part but are particularly concentrated in the Aravalli Hills which used to have a very dense forest cover but much of it has been destroyed in recent decades. They practise agriculture in small plots in the narrow hill valleys and hunt and trap small animals. Their main weapon is bow and arrow in the use of which they are highly proficient. The Kal Beliyas, Bagris, Bawarias, and Sansis are also found on both sides of the Aravallis but the Aheriyas, also known as Thoris, are mainly found in the western part. The Van Vagris are concentrated only in a few districts bordering the western side of the Aravallis. They live almost entirely by hunting and move in small bands of a few families. The Kal Beliyas are mainly snake catchers and charmers and are largely nomadic though some have been settled in exclusive colonies. The Bagris are engaged in agriculture. The Bawarias and Sansis are mainly engaged in criminal activities.

Rajasthan also has a long history of hunting-gathering way of life. In eastern Rajasthan Lower Palaeolithic sites are best known from the valleys of the Chambal, Banas and their tributaries and sub-tributaries like the Berach, Gambhiri, Wagan and Kadmali in Mewar. All the sites are in secondary context like the cemented gravels in cliffs or loose gravels in river beds. Some of them like those in the Gambhiri below the Chittaurgarh fort and in the Berach at Nagari are extraordinarily rich in the concentration of artefacts which include both early and late Acheulian types of bifaces. Typical Levallois flakes are found in the Gambhiri assemblage at Chittaurgarh. In the western part of the State equally rich early as well as late Acheulian assemblages are found from a number of primary context sites in the calcareous loam deposited in slow flowing streams or in playas around Didwana town in Nagaur district. In comparison Middle Palaeolithic sites are fewer in both regions. In the eastern part they are known from the Berach, Wagan and Kadmali valleys, and in the western part from many sites in the Luni valley, from a number of sites in the calcareous loam north of Didwana town, and one rich site buried in the fossil dune at Didwana.

Upper Palaeolithic sites are scarce in both regions, almost certainly because it was a period of extreme aridity.

However, arid conditions began to ameliorate towards the end of the Pleistocene following increase in rainfall. Evidence of increased rainfall is preserved in the dark clay deposits in salt lakes and in the deep brown weathering of the sand dunes. As a consequence plant and animal life registered a significant increase and with the availability of enhanced food resources human population witnessed a dramatic rise. This is eloquently reflected in the appearance of a large number of Mesolithic sites all over the State (Fig. 37). These sites occur mostly on the surface of and buried in sand dunes and there is hardly a dune on which at least a few microliths are not found. In the Mewar region these sites occur on rocky surfaces where raw material for making artefacts was available and along rivers on local sand dunes along the banks, as, for example, on the Kothari river at Bagor, Vagdana, and several other localities. There are other sites like Bujawar near Jodhpur, Tilwara, west of Balotra in Barmer district and Bagor in Bhilwara district which cover more than an acre and have dense concentration of microliths, associated scrapers, points, etc. and debitage. Excavations at Tilwara and Bagor and radiocarbon dates from the latter site show that the Mesolithic people at these sites were living a semi-sedentary and probably sedentary life.

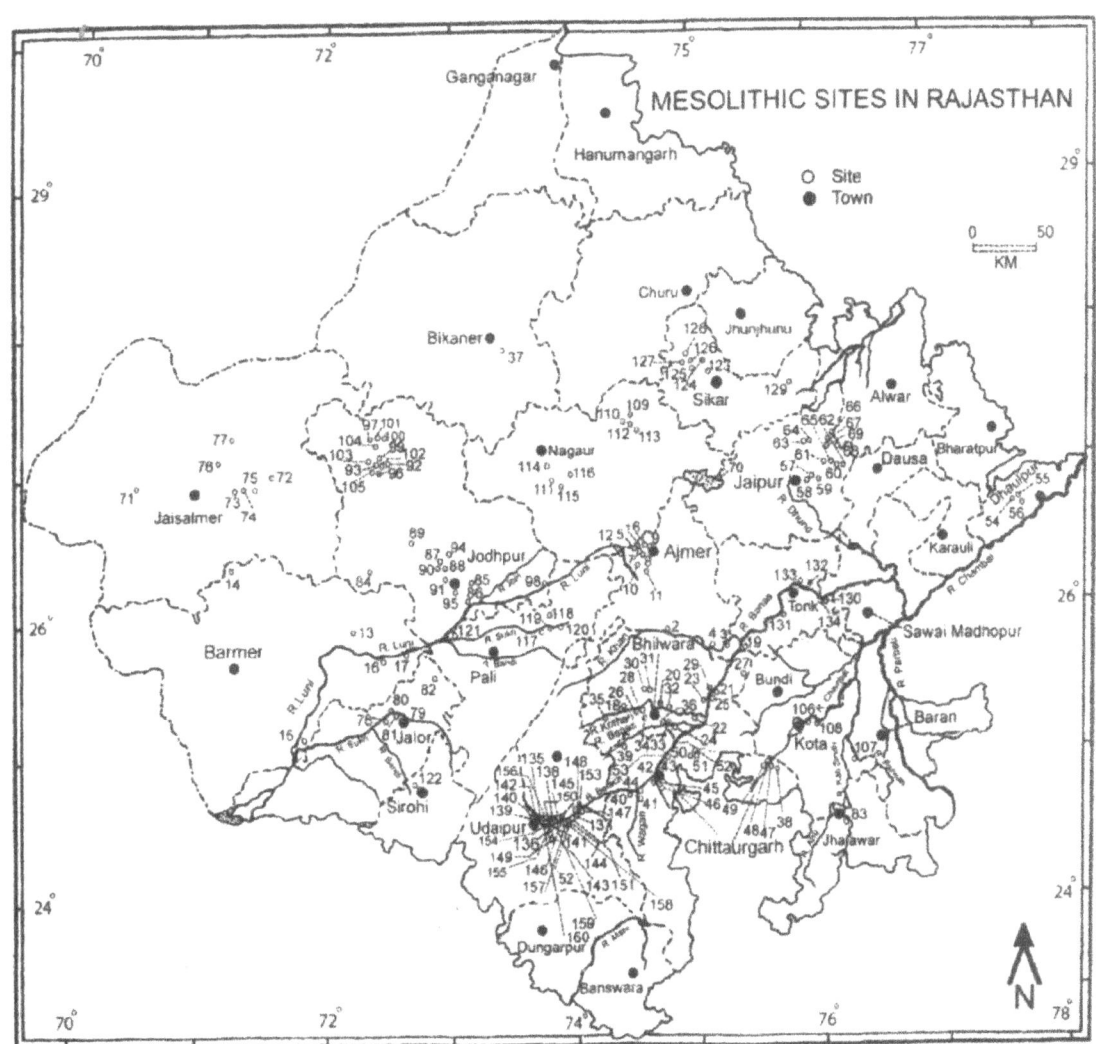

Fig. 37. Mesolithic sites in Rajasthan

Nomadic life is endemic in Rajasthan, particularly in the semi-arid and arid western part. Anyone travelling through the region cannot fail to notice small groups of people camping in makeshift shelters on sand dunes (Fig. 38). These people are hunter-gatherers like Van Vagris and Kal Beliyas, cattle traders like Banjaras, entertainers like Jogis and Bhopas and medicine dispensers like Moule Salam. These people stay at a place for a few days and then move on. The only vestiges of their occupation, which they leave behind, are the stones they used for making temporary hearths and for grinding spices, and some component of their silver or mixed metal ornaments or a metal tool like sickle or knife which they may have lost by accident. Such temporary camps of a few persons can be compared to Mesolithic occupations of a few people represented by small clusters of microliths and associated tools.

Fig. 38. A Banjara hut on a sand dune near Didwana

Like the Kanjars, the Van Vagris and Kal Beliyas also have large gatherings during community feasts to be given on the occasions of birth, death, marriage and worship of the clan goddess. On such occasions many clan members and affinal relatives are invited to take part in the feast. The relatives who come for such feasts may create a gathering of a hundred or more people. On such occasions food will be cooked on multiple *chulhas* or temporary ovens made of a few stones. There will be drinking of liquor and dancing if it is a happy occasion like birth or marriage. After the relatives have departed, the residue of their stay will comprise the remains of the *chulhas* or ovens and bones from which meat has been consumed, and any durable objects like an ornament, coin or metal tool which may have got lost by mistake and got buried in the sand. Such large gatherings, if repeated at the same site many times, will produce considerable refuse which can be compared to large Mesolithic sites like those of Bujawar, Tilwara, and Bagor. Excavations at Tilwara and Bagor and radiocarbon dates from the latter site show that the Mesolithic occupation at these sites covered areas of more than an acre and lasted over some five millennia, at least at Bagor.

Agriculture-based settled village life in the State first appeared in Mewar around five thousand years ago, and probably earlier, as revealed by the finds from the excavations at Ahar and Balathal in Udaipur district, Gilund in Rajsamand district, and Ojiyana and Lachhura in Bhilwara district, and radiocarbon dates from Balathal and Ahar. The pioneering farmers of the Ahar culture to which these sites belong, already had an economically and socially stratified society as revealed by the architecture and material culture. Some people lived in small one or two-roomed houses of wattle-and-daub while others lived in multi-roomed houses made of stone, mud and mud-brick. The settlements at Gilund, Balathal and Ojiyana were protected by boundary walls of stone, mud and mud-brick. At Balathal there was a large fortified enclosure made of stone, mud and mud-brick in the centre of the settlement. The Aharians had technologically and aesthetically rich and highly developed ceramics, a technology based mainly on copper, and ornaments of terracotta, semi-precious stones, copper, steatite and faience. They cultivated both summer and winter crops and evidently produced a surplus to be able to afford manpower for creating impressive public architecture.

Even though Aharian economy was based on agriculture, a certain amount of hunting continued as shown by the occurrence of bones of wild animals at all the excavated sites.

In the western part of the State agriculture-based life appeared probably around the same time as in Mewar but it was a consequence of diffusion from the Punjab which had received the knowledge earlier from Baluchistan. In the western part early agriculture was confined to the valley of the ancient Sarasvati (present-day dried-up Ghaggar) which was a perennially flowing river. The rest of the region was too dry to support agriculture until in the early medieval period pressure of population from outside pushed farmers into this area and technology had developed to sink deep wells to supply potable water. However, here cultivation was confined only to summer or *kharif* crop and the principal basis of subsistence was hunting-gathering and pastoralism.

Despite the long history of hunting-gathering all over the State and around five thousand year history of clearance of vegetation for agriculture over a sizable part wildlife comprising *nilgai*, *chinkara*, blackbuck, wild boar, hare, jackal, fox, porcupine, and monitor lizard, and many species of birds has survived even in the most arid parts. This in some measure is probably due to the strong respect for all life among most communities which in turn may be due to the influence of Jainism, Vaishya castes, and Bishnois, for the last of which conservation of animals and plants is religion.

6.3 Central India

Central India is even better endowed in resources for a hunting-gathering way of life than both Ganga Plains and Rajasthan. It receives good rainfall all over the region, has many perennial streams, and large areas under forest cover even to this day. Wildlife used to be abundant until even a few decades ago but pressure of population and illegal hunting has taken a heavy toll. The presence of many species of deer, antelope, gaur, buffalo, tiger and leopard in national parks and sanctuaries like Kanha-Kisli and Bandhavgarh gives a fair idea of its richness in the past.

There are many tribal communities like the Gonds, Baigas, Korwas, Cheros, Kamars, Khairwars, and Korkus which, while engaged in primitive plough or slash-and-burn cultivation, also practise hunting-gathering in varying degrees. Besides, communities like the Pardhis and Kuchbandhias live largely by hunting and only a few of their members are beginning to take to agriculture and settle down. Their economic and social interaction with Hindu caste groups provides excellent insight into the process by which hunting-gathering communities have been assimilated into the Hindu society.

The hunting-gathering history of central India is much richer than that of the Ganga plains and Rajasthan. Rich Lower Palaeolithic assemblages have been found in stratified Pleistocene deposits at many localities in the Narmada valley in Hoshangabad and Narsinghpur districts, including in the excavation at Mahadeo Piparia and Durkadi Nala. They have also been found in the valleys of the Chambal and Son and their tributaries as well as in excavation at the site of Sihawal in the Son valley in Sidhi district, and in rock shelter deposits at Bhimbetka in Sehore district. Besides, there are numerous surface sites as at Barkhera near Bhimbetka and at Putli Karar in Raisen district which have dense clusters of Acheulian artefacts. These clusters must be a product of the camping of large groups of hunter-gatherers over a prolonged period. The artefacts at all these sites are made exclusively of quartzite.

Middle Palaeolithic assemblages have been found in stratified context in excavation at Patpara in the Son valley and at Bhimbetka. They are also made of quartzite, and comprise a variety of scrapers, denticulates, notches, points, borers, and Levallois and discoid flakes and cores. The evidence for Upper Palaeolithic is comparatively scarce.

At Bhimbetka there is a distinct Upper Palaeolithic deposit. The artefacts, made of quartzite, comprise Levallois flakes, blades, scrapers, points, and microblades. They are much smaller than those of the Middle Palaeolithic. A Late Upper Palaeolithic assemblage is known from the site of Baghor in the Son valley. Here the artefacts are made of flinty chert and comprise long slender blades, scrapers, points, etc. An interesting discovery at this site was of several pieces of stones with coloured concentric bands as a part of a circular rubble platform. . When these were joined, they produced a triangular shape which the Baiga tribal workers at the site recognized as representing Kalaka Mata (Mother goddess). This appears to be the oldest evidence of a shrine in India.

As in the Ganga plains, Rajasthan, and many other parts of India, the evidence for Mesolithic is extremely rich in central India as well (Fig. 39). It comes mainly from the rockshelters at Bhimbetka and one rockshelter at Ghagharia in the Son valley. It consists of a highly developed geometric microlithic industry made of siliceous rocks like chert, chalcedony and jasper along with a small proportion of quartzite microblades. A number of human burials were found within the habitation deposit in at least three shelters at Bhimbetka. The body was placed in an extended position, and provided with grave goods in the form of grinding stones, bone tools, pieces of antler, and haematite nodules with tell-tale ground facets. There can be little doubt that the pigment from these nodules was used in the execution of paintings which decorate the walls, ceilings and niches of the shelters.

The paintings are in red, white and green colours and depict scenes of wildlife, hunting of animals by individual hunters, as well as groups of them, animals grazing, standing, moving, and frolicking, and composite animals combining features of several animals like bull and boar and displaying ferocity and inspiring a feeling of awe. These last appear to be depictions of animals which were probably worshipped as divinities. Besides, there are scenes of collection of fruits and honey from trees, fishing, digging of rats from ratholes and storing them in a bag, and scenes of what appear to be religious, ritual or social activities, like a man treating a patient or a group of people sitting in a hut. Later paintings, which are superimposed on the older ones, depict battle scenes with people fighting with swords and shields, spears, bow and arrows, men riding caparisoned horses and elephants, and moving in processions, and a royal figure moving under an umbrella.

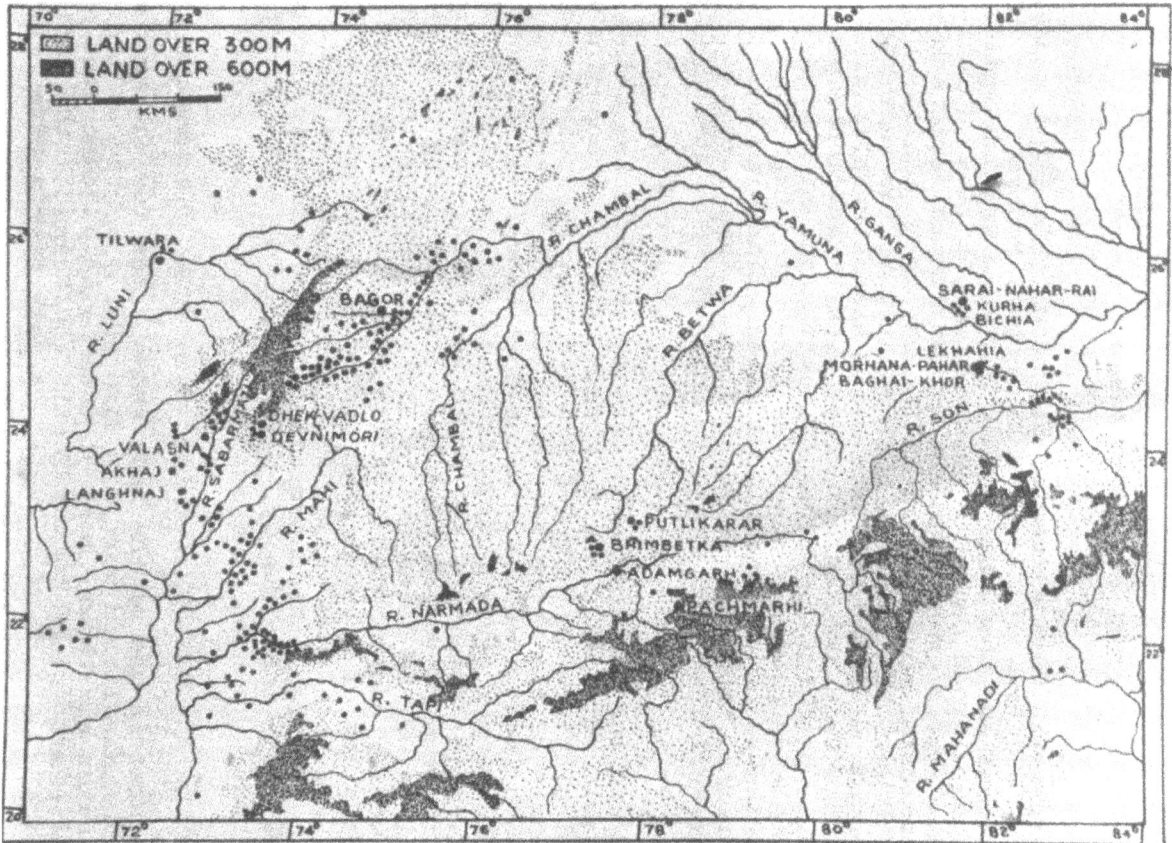

Fig. 39. Mesolithic sites in Central India

While small scatters of microliths found on the floor and outside the mouth of many shelters would represent a temporary occupation by a few individuals, rockshelters like IIB-33 with nearly 1.5 m thick habitation deposit, dense concentration of stone artefacts, and several human burials, would represent a sedentary or semi-sedentary occupation by the same or different human groups over at least a few decades, may be centuries. The existence of a few thousand paintings in scores of shelters also suggests that hunter-gatherers were staying here over long periods rather than visiting the site occasionally. The abundance of plant and animal food resources and the availability of water in *nullahs* during at least eight months of the year would make semi-sedentary life perfectly possible.

BIBLIOGRAPHY

Ansari, S. 2000. Small game hunting among the Musahars: An ethnoarchaeological approach, *Puratattva* 30:142-150.

Ansari, S. 2002. Fishing among the Mallahs of Allahabad district, Uttar Paradesh, *Man and Environment* 26(1): 39-55

Ansari, S. 2005. *Ethnoarchaeology of Prehistoric Settlement Pattern of South-Central Ganga valley.* Pune: Indian Society for prehistoric and Quaternary Studies.

Ayyangar, A. 1951. *Criminal Tribes Act Enquiry Committee, 1949-50.* New Delhi: Manager of Publications.

Beverley, H. 1872. *Report on the Census of Bengal, 1872.* Calcutta.

Bhargava, B.S. 1949. *The Criminal Tribes.* Lucknow.

Bhargava, B.S. 1950. *Tribes of India.* New Delhi: Bharatiya Adimjati Sevak Sangh.

Bhattacharya, J. N. 1896. *Hindu Castes and Sects.* Vols. I-II. Calcutta.

Binford, L.R. 1978. *Nunamiut Ethnoarchaeology.* New York: Academic Press.

Blunt, E.A.H. 1931. *The Caste System of Northern India.* London.

Bonnington, C.J. 1935. *Census of India, 1931, Vol. I: India, Part III: Ethnographic,* pp. 36-44. Simla.

Clark, J.D. and M.A.J. Williams 1990. prehistoric ecology, resource strategies and culture change in the Son Valley, Northern Madhya Pradesh, Central India, *Man and Environment* 15(1): 13-24.

Cline, E.A. 1967. Aheyreeahs, Memonrandum on the prevailing castes, *Census of the N. W. Provinces, 1865, Vol. I, General Report and Appendices.* Allahabad.

Cooper, Z.M. 1986. The Kurukh Fishermen of Bastar District, Central India, *Eastern Anthropologist* 39(1): 1-20.

Cooper, Z.M. 1993. The origin of the Andaman Islanders: local myth and archaeological evidence, *Antiquity* LXVII (255): 394-399.

Cooper, Z.M. 1997. *Prehistory of the Chitrakot Falls, Central, India.* Pune: Ravish Publishers.

Crooke, W. 1896. *The Tribes and Castes of the North-Western Provinces and Oudh.* Vols. I-IV. Calcutta.

Das, A.K., B.K. Roy Chowdhury and M.K. Raha 1966. *Handbook on Scheduled Castes and Scheduled Tribes of West Bengal.* Calcutta: Tribal Welfare Department, Government of West Bengal.

Datta, J.N. 1922. *Census of India, 1921,* Vol. XX, Gwalior, Part I, Report and Tables. Gwalior.

Egerton, B. 1891. *Census of India, 1891,* Report on the Census of Ajmer Mewar. Calcutta.

Ehrenfels, U.R. Von. 1952. *The Kadars of Cochin.* Madras: University of Madras.

Elliot, H.M. 1869. *The Races of the North-Western Provinces of India.* London.

Enthoven, R.E. 1922. *Tribes and Castes of Bombay.* Bombay: Government Central Press.

Erskine, Major K.D. 1908. *Rajputana Gazetteers, Vol. II-A. The Mewar Residency.* Ajmer: Scottish Mission

Erskine, Major K.D. 1909. *Rajputana Gazetteers, Vol. III-A. The Western Rajputana States Residency and the Bikaner Agency.* Allahabad: Pioneer Press.

Fuchs, Stephen. 1969. Nomadic Tribes in the Plains of North India, *Journal of the Gujarat Research Society* XXX(2): 92-101.

Fuerer-Haimendorf, C. Von. 1943. *The Chenchus : Jungle Folk of the Deccan* London: Macmillan.

Gait, E.A. 1892. *Census of India, 1891,* Vol. I, Assam, Report. Shillong.

Gautam, M.K. 1983. Itinerant camping life to settled basti alliances: the mechanism of ethnic maintenance and social organisation of the Kanjars of North India, *Eastern Anthropologist* 36(1): 15-29.

Gondal, R.P. 1937. The Vargrant Castes of the Kotah State, *Proceedings of the Indian Science Congress* (Abstracts) XXIV(Part III): 335. Hyderabad.

Gould, R.A. 1969. Subsistence Behaviour Among the Western Desert Aborigines of Australia, *Oceania* 39: 251-274.

Gould, R.A. 1980. *Living Archaeology.* Cambridge: University Press.

Hutton, J.H. 1951. *Caste in India.* London: Oxford University Press.

Ibbetson, D.C. 1883. *Report on the Census of Punjab, 1881,* pp. 314, 316. Calcutta.

Ibbetson, Sir Denzil 1916. *Panjab Castes.* Lahore: Punjab Government.

Jain, B.C. 1980. Tribal Panchayat of the Kajars of Moradabad City, *Indian Journal of Social Research* XXI(3): 188-189.

Jayaraj, J.S. 1983. *Early Hunter-Gatherer Adaptations in the Tirupati Valley, South India*. Ph.D. Thesis. Poona University.

Joglekar, P.P., V.D. Misra, J.N. Pal and M.C. Gupta 2003. *Mesolithic Mahadaha: The Faunal Remains*. Allahabad: Department of Ancient History, Culture and Archaeology, University of Allahabad.

Katiyar, T.S. 1964. *Social Life in Rajasthan*, pp. 50-52. Allahabad: Kitab Mahal.

Kaul, H.K. 1912. *Census of India, 1911,* Vol. XIV, Punjab, Part I, Report, pp. 461-462. Lahore.

Kennedy, K.A.R. 2000. *God-Apes and Fossil Men: Palaeoanthropology in South Asia*. Ann Arbor: Michigan University Press.

Kennedy, K.A.R., J.R. Lukacs, R.F. Pastor, T.L. Johnston, N.C. Lovell, J.N. Pal and C.B. Burrow 1992. Human Skeletal Remains from Mahadaha: A Gangetic Mesolithic Site. *Occasional Papers and Theses of the South Asia Program*. Cornell University. No. 11.

Kennedy, K.A.R., N.C. Lovell, and C.B. Burrow. 1986. Mesolithic Human Remains from the Gangetic Plain: Sarai Nahar Rai. *Occasional Papers and Theses of the South Asia Program*. Cornell University. No. 10.

Kirkpatrick, W. 1911. A vocabulary of the Pasi Boli or Argot of the Kunchbandiya Kanjars, *Journal of the Asiatic Society of Bengal* (New Series) VII(6): 277-287.

Kirkpatrick, W. 1911. Exogamous septs of the Gehara section of Kunchbandiya Kanjars, *Journal of the Asiatic Society of Bengal* (New Series) VII(10): 669-677.

Kirkpatrick, W. 1911. Folk-songs and Folk-lore of the Gehara (Kanjars), *Journal of the Asiatic Society of Bengal* (New Series) VII(7): 437- 442.

Kirkpatrick, W. 1911. Oaths and ordeals of the Geharas (Kanjars) of the Delhi District, *Journal of the Asiatic Society of Bengal* (New Series) VII(11): 753-756.

Kirkpatrick, W. 1913. Marriage ceremonies and marriage customs of the Gehara Kanjars (gypsy tribe), *Journal of the Asiatic Society of Bengal* (New Series) IX(1): 89-92.

Kitts, E.J. 1882. *Report on the Census of Berar, 1881*. Bombay.

Lal, B.B. 1997. *The Earliest Civilization of South Asia*. New Delhi: Aryan Books.

Lee, R.B. 1972. Work Effort, Group structure, and Land Use in Contemporary Hunter-Gatherers, in *Man, Settlement, and Urbanism* (P. Ucko, R. Tringham, and G.W. Dimbleby Eds.), pp. 177-185. London: Duckworth.

Lee, R.B. 1979. *The ! Kung San: Men, Women, and Work in a Foraging Society*. Cambridge: University Press.

Lee, R.B. and I. DeVore 1968. *Man the Hunter*. Chicago: Aldine.

Leeds, R.J. 1867. *Census of the North-Western Provinces, 1865, Vol. I: General Report and Appendices*. Allahabad.

Luiz, A.A.D. 1962. *The Tribes of Kerala*. New Delhi: Bharatiya Adimjati Sevak Sangh.

Lukacs, J.R. and J.N. Pal 1993. Mesolithic subsistence in north India: inferences from dental attributes, *Current Anthropology* 34(5): 745-765.

Maclagan, E.D. 1982. *Census of India, 1891,* Vol. XIX, Punjab and Its Feudatories, Part I, Report, pp. 306-307. Calcutta.

Mahalanobis, P.C., D.N. Majumdar and C.R. Rao 1946. Biometric analysis of anthropometric measurements on castes and tribes of the United Provinces, *Proceedings of the Indian Science Congress* (Abstracts), XXXIII, Part III, p. 138. Bangalore.

Majumdar, D.N. 1941-42. Blood groups of the criminal tribes of U.P., *Science and Culture* VII: 334-337.

Majumdar, D.N. 1944. *The Fortunes of Primitive Tribes*. Lucknow.

Majumdar, D.N. 1947. The criminal tribes of northern India, *Eastern Anthropologist* I(2): 33-40.

Malhotra, K.C., S.B. Khomne and M. Gadgil 1983. Hunting Strategies among Three Non-Pastoral Nomadic Groups of Maharashtra, *Man in India* 63(1): 21-39.

Mathur, U.B. 1969. *Ethnographic Atlas of Rajasthan (with reference to Scheduled Castes and Scheduled Tribes)*, Census of India 1961: V, Rajasthan. Delhi: Manager of Publications.

Mathur, U.B. 1986. *Folkways in Rajasthan*. Jaipur: The Folklorists.

Meade, M. J. 1905. On the Moghias or Baoris of Rajputana and Central India, *Journal of the Anthropological Society of Bombay* 7: 169-190.

Meade, M.J. 1886. On the Moghias or Baoris of Rajputana and Central India, *Journal of the Anthropological Society of Bombay* I: 274-288.

Meena, R.B. and A. Tripathi 2000. Further excavations at Ojiyana, *Puratattva* 30: 67-73.

Meena, R.B. and A. Tripathi 2001. Further excavations at Ojiyana, *Puratattva* 31: 73-78.

Misra, B.B. 2006. Koldihwa: A key site for the Neolithic-Chalcolithic culture of the Vindhyas, In C.P. Sinha (Ed.), *Art, Archaeology and Cultural History of India*, pp. 143-181. Delhi: B.R. Publishers.

Misra, V.D. 1977. *Aspects of Indian Archaeology*. Allahabad: Prabhat Prakashan.

Misra, V.D. 2007. Stone Age cultures, their chronology and beginnings of agriculture in north-central India, *Man and Environment*. 32(1): 1-14.

Misra, V.D., J.N. Pal and M.C. Gupta 2001. Excavations at Tokwa: A Neolithic-Chalcolithic settlement, *Pragdhara* 11: 59-72.

Misra, V.N. 1971. Two Mesolithic sites in Rajasthan: A preliminary investigation, *The Eastern Anthropologist* 24(3): 237-288.

Misra, V.N. 1973. Bagor – A Late Mesolithic site in northwest India, *World Archaeology* 5(1): 92-110.

Misra, V.N. 1976. Evidence of culture contact between terminal stone age hunter-gatherers and contemporary farmers, In *Archaeological Congress and* Seminar (U.V. Singh Ed.), pp. 115-121. Kurukshetra: Kurukshetra University.

Misra, V.N. 1990. The Van Vagris: "Lost" Hunters of the Thar Desert, Rajasthan, *Man and Environment* 15(2): 89-108.

Misra, V.N. 2007. *Prehistoric and Early Historic Foundations of Rajasthan* New Delhi: Aryan Books International.

Misra, V.N. and S.N. Rajaguru 1989. Palaeoenvironment and prehistory in the Thar desert, Rajasthan, India, In *South Asian Archaeology 1985* (Karen Frifelt and Per Sorensen Eds.), pp. 296-320. Copenhagen: Scandinavian Institute of Asian Studies.

Murty, M.L.K. 1981a. Hunter-Gatherer Ecosystems and Archaeological Patterns of Subsistence Behaviour on the Southeast Coast of India: An Ethnographic Model, *World Archaeology* 13(1): 47-58.

Murty, M.L.K. 1981b. Symbiosis and Traditional Behaviour in the Subsistence Economics of the Kanchapuri Yerukulas of South India: A Predictive Model, *Puratattva* 10: 50-61.

Nagar, M. 1982. Fishing Among the Tribal Communities of Bastar and Its Implications for Archaeology, *Bulletin of the Deccan College Research Institute*.

Nagar, M. 1985a. The Use of Wild Plant Foods by Aboriginal Communities in Central India, in *Recent Advances in Indo-Pacific Prehistory* (V.N. Misra and P. Bellwood Eds.), pp. 337-342. New Delhi: Oxford-IBH.

Nagar, M. 1985b. Ethnoarchaeology of the Bhimbetka region, *Man and Environment* 7: 61-69.

Nagar, M. and V.N. Misra 1990. Kanjars: A Hunting-Gathering community of the Ganga valley, Uttar Pradesh, *Man and Environment* 15(2): 71-88.

Nagar, M. and V.N. Misra 1993. The Pardhis: A Hunting-Gathering community of central and eastern India. *Man and Environment* 18(1): 115-140.

Nagar, M. and V.N. Misra 1989. Hunter-gatherers in an agrarian setting: The nineteenth century situation in the Ganga plains, *Man and Environment* 13: 17-64.

Nanda, S.C. 1984. *Stone Age Cultures of Indravati Basin, Koraput District Orissa*. Ph.D. Thesis, Poona University.

Nanda, S.C. 1985. The Mesolithic culture of the Indravati valley, district Koraput, Orissa, In, *Recent Advances in Indo-Pacific Prehistory* (V.N. Misra and P. Bellwood Eds.), pp. 159-163. New Delhi: Oxford-IBH.

Nesfield, John C. 1883. The Kanjars of Upper India, *Calcutta Review* LXXVII: 368-398.

Pal, J.N. 1984. Epi-Palaeolithic Sites in Pratapgarh District, Uttar Pradesh, *Man and Environment* 8: 31-38.

Pal, J.N. 1985. Some New Light on the Mesolithic Burial Practices of the Ganga Valley: Evidence from Mahadaha, Pratapgarh, Uttar Pradesh, *Man and Environment* 9: 28-37.

Pal, J.N. 1988. Mesolithic double burials from recent excavations at Damdama, *Man and Environment* 12: 115-122..

Pal, J.N. 1994. Mesolithic settlements in the Gangetic plain, north India, *Man and Environment* 19 (1-2): 97-102.

Plowden, W.C. 1883. *Report of the Census of British India, 1881*, Vol. I. London.

Raju, D.R. 1988. *Stone Age Hunter-Gatherers: An Ethno-Archaeology of Cuddapah Region South-East India.* Pune: Ravish Publishers.

Risley, H.H. 1891. *The Tribes and Castes of Bengal,* Vol. I. Calcutta.

Risley, H.H. 1901. *The People of India.* London.

Rose, H.A. 1911. *A Glossary of the Tribes and Castes of the Punjab & N.W.F.P.* Vols. II-III. Lahore.

Roy, S.C. 1925. *Birhors, a Little Known Jungle Tribe of Chota Nagpur.* Ranchi: Man in India.

Russell, R.V. and R.B. Hira Lal 1916. *Tribes and Castes of the Central Provinces of India.* Vols. I-IV. London: Macmillan & Co.

Saksena, H.S. 1975. Denotified communities of Uttar Pradesh in perspective, *Indian Anthropologist* 5(1): 1-10.

Sangave, V.A. 1967. Phanse Pardhis of Kolhapur: A Tribe in Transition, *Sociological Bulletin* XVI: 81-88.

Shah, Vimal 1968. *Gujarat ke Adivasi.* Ahmedabad: Gujarat Vidyapeeth.

Shakespear, J. 1818. Observations regarding Badhiks and Thags from an official report dated the 30th April, 1816, *Asiatic Researches* 13: 282-292.

Sharma, G.R. 1973. Mesolithic lake cultures in the Ganga valley, India, *Proceeding of the Prehistoric Society* XXXIX: 129-156.

Sharma, G.R. and J.D. Clark (Eds.) 1983. *Palaeoenvironments and Prehistory in the Middle Son Valley, Madhya Pradesh, Central India.* Allahabad: University of Allahabad.

Sharma, G.R., V.D. Misra, D. Mandal, B.B. Misra and J.N. Pal 1980. *Beginnings of Agriculture.* Allahabad: Abinash Prakashan.

Sharma, P. 1959. Nomadic Tribes of Rajasthan, *Journal of Social Research Rajasthan* I(2): 21-28.

Sherring, M.A. 1872. *Hindu Tribes and Castes as represented in Benaras.* Vols. I-III. Calcutta.

Singh, G., R.D. Joshi, S.K. Chopra and A.B. Singh 1974. Late Quaternary History of Vegetation and Climate of the Rajasthan Desert, India, *Philosophical Transactions of the Royal Society* 267B: 467-501.

Sollas, W.J. 1924. *Ancient Hunters and Their Modern Representatives.* London: MacMillan and Co. Ltd.

Temple, R.C. 1882. Folklore in the Panjab, *The Indian Antiquary* XI: 42.

Tewari, R., R.K. Srivastava, K.K. Singh, K.S. Saraswat and I.B. Singh 2003. Preliminary Report of the Excavation at Lahuradewa, District Sant Kabir Nagar, U.P. – 20001-2002. Wider Archaeological Implications, *Pragdhara* 13: 37-68.

Tewari, R., R.K. Srivastava, K.K. Singh, Ram Vinay, R.K. Trivedi and G.C. Singh 2005. Recently excavated sites in the Ganga plain and North Vindhyas: some observations regarding the pre-urban context, *Pragdhara* 15: 37-68.

The Maharashtra Census Office. 1972. *Scheduled Tribes in Maharashtra Ethnographic Notes.* Census of India 1961, X, Maharashtra, Part V-B, Delhi: Manager of Publications.

Thomas, P.K. 1984. Role of Animals in the Food Economy of the Mesolithic Cultures of Western and Central India, in, *Archaeozoological Studies* (A.T. Clason Ed.), pp. 322-328. Amsterdam: North Holland Publishing Co.

Thomas, P.K., P.P. Joglekar, V.D. Misra, J.N. Pandey and J.N. Pal 2002. Faunal Remains from Damdama: Evidence for the Mesolithic Food Economy of the Gangetic Plain, In, *Mesolithic India* (V.D. Misra and J.N. Pal Eds.), pp. 366-380. Allahabad: Department of Ancient History, Culture and Archaeology, University of Allahabad.

Turner, A.C. 1933. *Census of India, 1931, Vol. XVIII: United Provinces of Agra & Oudh, Part I: Report.* Allahabad.

Varma, R.K., V.D. Misra, J.N. Pandey and J.N. Pal 1985. A Preliminary Report on the Excavations at Damdama (1982-84), *Man and Environment* 9: 45-65.

Wahi, L.N. 1949. The Bhantus, a criminal tribe in the United Provinces, *Man in India* 29: 84-91.

Wasson, R.J., G.I. Smith and D.P. Agrawal 1984. Late Quaternary Sediments, Minerals and Inferred Geochemical History of Didwana Lake, Thar Desert, India, *Palaeogeography, Palaeoclimatology, Palaeoecology* 46: 345-372.

White, J.P. 1967. Ethno-Archaeology in New Guinea: Two Examples, *Mankind* 6: 409-414.

William, J.C. 1869. *Report on the Census of Oudh, 1869, Vol. II: Appendices and Statistical Tables,* Lucknow.

Yellen, J.E. 1977. *Archaeological Approaches to the Present: Models for Reconstructing the Past.* London: Academic Press.

About Author

Dr. Malti Nagar did her M.A. in Anthropology from Lucknow University with specialization in Social Anthropology in 1958 and in Prehistoric Anthropology in 1962. Later she did her Ph.D. in Archaeology in 1967 from Poona University under the guidance of the eminent archaeologist, H.D. Sankalia, on the topic: Ahar Culture: An Ethnoarchaeological Study. For her doctoral research she carried out a detailed study of the excavated material from the Chalcolithic site of Ahar and extensive field work among the Bhils, a tribal community living in villages of Udaipur and adjoining districts of Mewar as well as among the farming and artisan castes of the same region.

Dr. Nagar worked as a Research Assistant in the Archaeology Department of the Deccan College, Pune from 1966 to 1972, and was appointed as Lecturer in Ethnoarchaeology in the same Department in 1973, the first position in this discipline to be created in an Indian University. She was appointed as a Reader in Asian Archaeology in the same Department in 1988.

Dr. Nagar has carried out field work among the Maria Gonds of Bastar, Chhattisgarh, the Bhils in Gujarat; the Bhils, Sansis and Kal Beliyas in Rajasthan; the Pardhis and Kuchbandhias in Madhya Pradesh; the Birhors in Jharkhand, the Kanjars in Uttar Pradesh, and the Bondos in Orissa. Her work on the ethnoarchaeology of the Bhimbetka area in M.P. and on the use of wild plant foods by the Gonds and other tribal communities in Bastar is specially significant. She has published a large number of research papers in the *Eastern Anthropologist, Man and Environment, Journal of the Deccan College Post-Graduate and Research Institute, Indian Antiquary* and in edited volumes in India and abroad.

Dr. Nagar is a life member of the Ethnographic and Folk Culture Society, Lucknow, Indian archaeological Society, New Delhi, and Indian Society for Prehistoric and Quaternary Studies (ISPQS), Pune. She has been a member of the Executive Committee of ISPQS for several years. She is a regular participant in the annual conference of the Indian Archaeological Society and ISPQS. She also participated in the conference of the Indo-Pacific Prehistory Association at Osaka and Tokyo in 1987 and in the International Symposium on the ethnoarchaeology of South Asia at Cambridge in 1991.

SOUTH ASIAN ARCHAEOLOGY SERIES

EDITED BY ALOK K. KANUNGO

SAA No 1. Kanungo, Alok Kumar 2004 *Glass Beads in Ancient India: An Ethnoarchaeological Approach* (*British Archaeological Reports, International Series* S1242) Oxford. ISBN 1 84171 364 3.

SAA No 2. Kanungo, Alok Kumar (Ed) 2005 *Gurudakshina: Facets of Indian Archaeology, Essays presented to Prof. V.N. Misra* (*British Archaeological Reports, International Series* S1433) Oxford. ISBN 1 84171 723 1.

SAA No 3. Swayam, S. 2006 *Invisible People: Pastoral life in Proto-Historic Gujurat* (*British Archaeological Reports, International Series* S1464) Oxford. ISBN 1 84171 732 0.

SAA No 4. Mushrif-Tripathy, Veena & Walimbe S.R. 2006 *Human Skeletal Remains from Chalcolithic Nevasa: Osteobiographic Analysis* (*British Archaeological Reports, International Series* S1476) Oxford. ISBN 1 84171 737 1.

SAA No 5. Jahan, Shahnaj Husne 2006 *Excavating Waves and Winds of (Ex)change: A Study of Maritime Trade in Early Bengal* (*British Archaeological Reports, International Series* S1533) Oxford. ISBN 1 84171 753 3.

SAA No 6. Pawankar, Seema J. 2007 *Man and Animal Relationship in Early Farming Communities of Western India, with Special Reference to Inamgaon* (*British Archaeological Reports, International Series* S1639) Oxford. ISBN 978 1 4073 0062 7.

SAA No 7. Sharma, Sukanya 2007 *Celts, Flakes and Bifaces – The Garo Hills Story* (*British Archaeological Reports, International Series* S1664) Oxford. ISBN 978 1 4073 0068 9.

SAA No 8. Kanungo, Alok Kumar (Ed) 2007 *Gurudakshina: Facets of Indian Archaeology, Essays presented to Prof. V.N. Misra* (Part II) (*British Archaeological Reports, International Series* S1665) Oxford. ISBN 978 1 4073 0069 6.

SAA No 9. Nagar, Malti 2008 Hunter-Gatherers in North and Central India: An Ethnoarchaeological Study (*British Archaeological Reports, International Series* S1749) Oxford. ISBN 978 1 4073 0209 6.

www.ingramcontent.com/pod-product-compliance
Lightning Source LLC
Chambersburg PA
CBHW061543010526
44113CB00023B/2780